CISTERCIAN STUDIES SERIES: NUMBER TWENTY-THREE

ALAN OF LILLE

THE ART OF PREACHING

ALAN OF LILLE

CISTERCIAN STUDIES SERIES: NUMBER TWENTY-THREE

THE ART OF PREACHING

TRANSLATED, WITH AN INTRODUCTION
BY GILLIAN R. EVANS

CISTERCIAN PUBLICATIONS, INC.
Kalamazoo, Michigan
1981

A translation of Alanus de Insulis, *Ars praedicandi,*
from the Latin text in J.-P. Migne, *Patrologia cursus
completus, series latina,* Volume 210, columns 109–135.

Library of Congress Cataloguing in Publication Data

Alanus de Insulis, d. 1202.
  The art of preaching.

  (Cistercian Fathers series ; no. 23)
  Translation of Ars praedicandi, which was issued
in v. 210 of Patrologiae cursus completus, series
Latina.
  1. Preaching—Early works to 1800. I. Title.
BV4209.A4213 1981   251   80–24611
ISBN 0-87907-923-1

Composition by Gale Akins, Kalamazoo, Michigan
Cover design by Linda Hensley.
Printed in the United States of America

TABLE OF CONTENTS

ALAN OF LILLE,

THE ART OF PREACHING

THE INTRODUCTION

INTRODUCTION

LIFE AND WORKS

ALAN OF LILLE led a long life as scholar and religious. When his body was exhumed in 1960, it appeared that he had been well into his eighties when he died in 1202.[1] He was probably born at Lille in Flanders. Nothing is known of his early life, but he certainly studied at Paris as a young man, and perhaps at Chartres, in the years when some of the most important and influential masters of the first half of the twelfth century were teaching in the schools of northern France. Of these, perhaps Gilbert of Poitiers and Thierry of Chartres had the greatest influence on Alan, awakening his interest in some of the newly-fashionable works of the day, in particular, the theological tractates of Boethius and the work of Pseudo-Dionysius on the celestial hierarchy. In his turn, Alan himself taught at Paris, and probably at Montpellier, too. To judge from his title of *Doctor Universalis*, even in a scholarly milieu Alan passed for an exceptionally learned man.

It is likely that he came into contact with the Cistercians while he was in the south of France. They were actively engaged in missionary work in the Languedoc area, and Alan himself may have preached against the heretics there. The detailed treatment of the Cathar heresy in the first of his four books against the heretics suggests that he knew more about these latter-day Manichees than about the Waldensians, Jews, and Moslems to whom he devotes the other three books. At some time before his death, Alan entered Citeaux, as had Thierry of Chartres and a number of other scholars before him.

Alan wrote a great deal, and his works cover a wide range of literary and theological *genres*. Of the 'literary' pieces, the work which has received most attention from both mediaeval and modern commentators

is the *Anticlaudianus,* an epic poem in which Alan describes the
fashioning of the perfect man by Nature and the Virtues. He is to
restore the world to beauty and peace by living a perfect human life,
and defeating the Vices in battle. (Claudian wrote a poem depicting
Rufinus as a wholly evil man; Alan intends to portray his opposite in
the *Anticlaudianus,* and he chose his title as a playful reference to
Claudian's work). The same debt to Late Roman literature is notice-
able in the *De planctu naturae,* or *The Complaint of Nature,* which is
composed in alternating prose and verse, like Boethius' *Consolation of
Philosophy,* and which, like the *Anticlaudianus,* owes much to Martianus
Capella's *De nuptiis Philologiae et Mercurii.* In the *Consolation* Boethius
converses with Philosophy; in the *De planctu naturae* Alan talks to
Nature in a vision. Instead of Fortune he introduces Genius; instead of
Providence he takes Virtue as his subject.

Alan's works of speculative theology includes the *Summa quoniam
homines,* and the *Regulae theologicae.* The first of these was intended
to cover the range of material which was coming, during the course of
the twelfth century, to constitute a full syllabus of theology: the nature
of God, unity and Trinity, the creation of angels and man, redemption,
sacraments, the end of the world and the resurrection of the dead. The
Summa is incomplete, but in the *Regulae theologicae* Alan provides a
fuller conspectus of the subject-matter of speculative theology. He does
so in an unusual way. In Boethius' *De hebdomadibus* a system of
axiomatic demonstration is proposed. Boethius gives nine maxims, and
suggests that his readers will be able to apply them for themselves to his
argument about the way in which substances can be good simply by
virtue of their existence, without being absolute good. As a number of
twelfth century commentators point out, it is by no means easy to apply the maxims. Alan has adapted the idea; he extends the nine maxims
to 134 *Regulae* and attempts to demonstrate the whole of Christian
doctrine by this axiomatic method. The inspiration is ultimately
Euclidean, but Alan's immediate source is undoubtedly Boethius, and
only in a limited sense can this be called a geometrical theology. Never-
the less, it is a most enterprising experiment in speculative theology,
which seems to have had no imitators, unless we count the more strictly
Euclidean work of Nicholas of Amiens, the *De arte catholicae fidei*

written at the end of the 1180s, and dedicated to Pope Clement III.

Alan wrote commentaries, on the *Song of Songs,* on the Apostle's Creed, on the Nicene Creed, and on the *Prosa de Angelis* which was used as a Sequence for Michaelmas. He composed four books against heretics, a dictionary of theological terms, a book on virtues and vices, another on the reasons why Mass is not to be celebrated twice on the same day, another on the sacrament of penance and another on the 'six wings of the cherubim' in *Isaiah 6:* 1-10, and many more.

The *Art of Preaching* and the *Sermons* (which will be published in a companion volume) are Alan's works of practical theology.

ALAN THE PREACHER

Alan's manual of preaching occupies a special place in the history of preaching. The homilies of the Fathers—in particular those of Augustine and Gregory—had long supplied the needs of monastic communities. Original sermons were so rarely preached that St Anselm's preaching and 'table-talk' aroused enthusiastic admiration because of their sheer novelty, as well as because of their excellence, when he spoke to the communities of the houses he visited on his travels.[1] Guibert of Nogent, a younger contemporary of St Anselm, composed a *Book on Making Sermons*[2] in which he discusses the motives which should lead a man to preach, the principles by which the preacher should be guided, the frame of mind in which he should address himself to the task ('Let prayer come before preaching').[3] Guibert remarks on the need for the preacher to adapt the sermon to the capacity of the audience: 'While he speaks to the simple plainly and simply, when he speaks to more learned men, let him add those deeper matters which are suitable for their ears'.[4] His treatise covers much the same ground as Alan's prefatory remarks in the *Art of Preaching.*

But Alan wrote, a century later, within a scholarly milieu rather different from that in which Guibert lived and worked. The sermons of Stephen Langton and Peter the Chanter,[5] demonstrate that method and principle had become considerably more technical in the intervening years. Doctrinal and theological themes join the often more homely subject matter of the patristic homilies, which are concerned with the practical living of the Christian life. From 1230–1 the Art of Preaching

was to become a highly formal art.[6] The university-style sermon took a
theme, usually (if not always) a text of Scripture, and divided it. The
preacher tried to win his audience's attention and interest with a
protheme, in which he might invite his listeners to pray with him.
This served the same purpose as the 'securing of good-will' (*captatio
benevolentiae*) of the Art of Letter-Writing. The theme proper was
then introduced and expounded in a narrative or a sequence of argu-
mentation. It was divided into three parts, often labelled by terms
which rhymed, so as to aid the memory of the listeners. In expounding
these, and any further subdivisions of the subject which could be drawn
out of the theme, a variety of rhetorical devices was employed:
digressio, correspondentia, circulatio, unitio, convolutio, for example.
The Art of Preaching, then, at its most fully developed, satisfied the
scholastic desire for order, exactness, and meticulousness. Several
features of Alan's method, especially in the *Sermons* themselves, suggest that the manuals of the thirteenth century formalised a method of
preaching which had already been well-tried in practice. Alan's manual
occupies an intermediate position of some importance. It is an explana-
tion of the theory of sermon composition which was developing in the
schools and monasteries of the late twelfth century. The collections of
material for the preacher arranged under topics include some division
of the subject, and in the sermons themselves, a Scriptural *thema* is often
divided and treated in a manner worthy of the thirteenth century art.
A wide range of examples provides illustration.

THE TEXT
    There is no modern edition of the *Art of Preaching*. The only printed
text is that of C. de Visch, which is reproduced in J.P. Migne *Patrologia
Latina* 210, cols. 109–95. It is upon this edition that this translation
has been based, for the convenience of readers who wish to refer to an
easily accessible Latin text. The Migne text is far from satisfactory,
however, and its use as a basis for translation requires some justifica-
tion.
    C. de Visch made use of two manuscripts, one of which contains
the whole of the *Art of Preaching*, while the other ends at Chapter 30.
The first of these is now in the municipal library at Bruges (MS 193);

the other is now Bruges 222. In 1951 G. Raynaud de Lage published
a list of more than ninety manuscripts of the *Art of Preaching*.[1] A number of these were examined by M. T. d'Alverny in preparing her edition
of some of Alan's Sermons.[2] She came to the conclusion that one
group of four manuscripts—Paris Bib. nat. n. acq. lat. 335; Dijon 211;
Munich CLM 4616, and Vatican, Reg. Christinae lat. 424—might provide
an acceptable basis for an edition,[3] but the manuscript tradition is complex, and it would seem premature to embark upon any attempt at
editing without examining the remaining manuscripts. The task is a
major one, not only because of the number of manuscripts involved,
but also because of the nature of the work. The *Art of Preaching* was
intended to be used as a practical manual. It was a popular work, and
copyists anxious to provide copies in a hurry sometimes worked care-
lessly. And it lends itself to the insertion of additional material or the
omission of portions of the text, to changes in the chapter-headings,
to abbreviation or extension. It would be difficult to establish Alan's
intentions with any confidence.

It is possible, as M. T. d'Alverny suggests, that the work was composed in stages. One group of manuscripts ends, like MS Bruges 222,
at Chapter 30. There is a natural division of the subject-matter into
three: an introductory essay in which Alan outlines the theory of the
art of preaching, and which is further subdivided under headings in some
manuscripts ('On avoiding scurrility in preaching'; 'On the form of
preaching', MS Add.18325, British Library; 'What preaching is and
what it ought to be', MS Cott. Vesp. D XIII, British Library, for example). This is followed by a series of chapters on such subjects as
'despising the world', 'despising oneself', 'gluttony', 'avarice', 'envy',
and running on to the chapter on 'hospitality', which is Chapter 37 in
the Migne text. MS Cott. Vesp. D.XIII distinguishes these chapters with
an *informacio ad*, throughout. At the end of the preface Alan explains
that it is important that the preacher should make use of examples, and
there is every reason to suppose that he intended the chapters which
follow to provide collections of authorities and ready-made examples as a
starting-point for preachers. If Mlle d'Alverny is right in thinking that the
manuscripts which end at Chapter 30 represents Alan's first version, then
this series, or that part of it which is to be found in these manuscripts,

(for the final chapters are missing) constitutes a self-contained *Art* of preaching in its own right.

There follows, in the longer versions, a series of chapters explaining that the question 'what is preaching?' has now been answered (and 'what is preaching like?' and 'what should preaching be about?'). It remains, says Alan, to show who the preacher should be, and to whom preaching should be given or delivered (PL 210:182, 184). Alan had indicated in his Prologue that the mastery of the Art of Preaching involved all these things, and these final chapters, on how to preach to soldiers, princes, monks, widows, and so on, are clearly in keeping with his original intention, whether or not they were added at a later stage, after the first thirty chapters or so were already in circulation.

In the present state of knowledge, then, Migne provides us with no more than a working text, and the translation which has been based on it pretends to be nothing more than an English working text. It is unlikely that a definitive edition will be available in the foreseeable future. In the meantime it is important that a treatise of such unusual interest for the early history of the Art of Preaching should not be neglected, and it is hoped that the present version will provide a starting-point for further work.

A group of twenty-seven sermons for the liturgical year is sometimes found with the *Art of Preaching*. This *Liber Sermonum* was perhaps intended to serve much the same purpose as the collections of pattern-letters which often accompany manuals on the Art of Letter-Writing of the twelfth century and later. Some of these sermons are found independently elsewhere, in longer or shorter form, as though Alan himself had used them on more than one occasion, and adapted them. [These sermons will appear shortly in a companion volume—ed.]

SOURCES AND CITATIONS

Of the sources on which Alan draws in the *Art of Preaching* and *Sermons,* the prime authority, as we should expect, is Holy Scripture. In each chapter of the *Art of Preaching* Alan lists first the biblical texts he recommends to his preacher as possible themes, and then a series of patristic texts, followed sometimes by an appropriate secular authority. The books of the Bible on which Alan draws most consistently, the

Sapiential Books, the Psalms, the Gospels, present no surprises. Among patristic writers, Alan leans most heavily upon Augustine, Gregory and Jerome, with Bede, and Isidore. Secular writers are represented by Boethius, Cicero, Claudian, Horace, Juvenal, Ovid, Macrobius, Seneca, Statius, Virgil, and citations of 'Aristotle', 'Plato' and 'Socrates'. Although Alan was exceptionally well-read, there seems no doubt that he made use of *florilegia*[1] in compiling his collection of quotations, and that the quotations were often drawn ready-made from existing compilations, rather than taken directly from their sources.

NOTES TO INTRODUCTION

SECTION I: LIFE AND WORKS
1. M. Lebeau 'Découverte du tombeau du bienheureux Alain de Lille' *Collectanea* 23 (1961) 254-60. The evidences for Alan's life, details and discussions of manuscripts and full bibliographies are given in *Textes*, and J.J. Sheridan adds some recent publications in his account of Alan's works in *Alan of Lille: Anticlaudianus* (Toronto 1973).

SECTION 2: ALAN THE PREACHER
1. *Memorials of St. Anselm* ed. R. W. Southern and F. S. Schmitt (London, 1969) Introduction, and R. W. Southern *St. Anselm and his Biographer* (Cambridge 1966) p. 226.
2. PL 156:21-32.
3. PL 156:24, cf. Augustine *De doctrina christiana* IV.xv.32,IV.xxx.63.
4. PL 156:25.
5. On Petrus Cantor, whose *Verbum Abbreviatum* affords some interesting parallels with AP, see *Textes* p. 148-51, and on Stephen Langton's sermons, see P. B. Roberts *Studies in the Sermons of Stephen Langton* (Toronto 1973).
6. For the development of this art, see the studies listed in J. J. Murphy *Bibliography of Mediaeval Rhetoric* (Toronto 1971) 40-1.

SECTION 3: THE TEXT
1. G. Raynaud de Lage *Alain de Lille: Poète du xiie siècle* (Paris 1951) pp. 179-82.
2. M. T. d'Alverny *Alain de Lille: Textes inédits* (Paris 1965) 109-148.
3. Ibid. pp. 112-3.
4. *Textes* p. 112.

SECTION 4: SOURCES AND CITATIONS
1. The following collections of *florilegium* material contain items to be found in Alan of Lille's pastoral writings:
Ps–Caecilius Balbus *De nugis philosophorum* ed. E. Woellflin (Basle

1855); William of Conches *Moralium dogma philosophorum* ed. G. Holmberg (Uppsala 1929); Otloh of St Emmeram *Libellus Proverbiorum,* ed. G. C. Korfmacher (Chicago 1936); *Florilegium morale Oxoniense; Analecta Medievalia Namurcensia* 6 (Louvain 1956); *I Collectanea di Eirico di Auxerre;* ed. I. Quadri *Spicilegium Friburgense* 11 (Freiburg 1966).

THE ART OF PREACHING

[PL 210:111] ## THE AUTHOR'S PREFACE

Gn 28:12

JACOB BEHELD A LADDER reaching from earth to heaven, on which angels were ascending and descending.'[1] The ladder represents the progress of the catholic man in his ascent from the beginning of faith to the full development of the perfect man. The first rung of this ladder is confession; the second, prayer; the third, thanksgiving; the fourth, the careful study of the Scriptures; the fifth, to inquire of someone more experienced[2] if one comes upon any point in Scripture which is not clear; the sixth, the expounding of Scripture; the seventh, preaching.[3]

The man who repents his sin then should first set his foot on the first rung of this ladder by confessing his sin. He should mount to the second rung by praying to God that grace may be bestowed on him. The third rung is reached through thanksgiving for the grace which is given. The ascent to the fourth rung is made by studying Scripture so as to preserve the gift of grace—for Holy Scripture teaches how grace, once

1.   Jacob's ladder provides many writers with similar analogies. See, for example, RB c.7.
2.   Or: 'a greater authority', perhaps one of the patristic commentators?
3.   Compare the seven *modi* of preaching and the seven qualities of the preacher distinguished in two of the *artes* described by H. Caplan 'Classical Rhetoric and the Mediaeval Theory of Preaching' *Classical Philology* 28 (1933) 73-96.

given, may be held fast. In this way the fifth rung is seen in sight, when a doubtful point arises, and the reader asks someone senior to help him understand it. The sixth rung is reached when the reader himself expounds Holy Scripture to others. He climbs the seventh rung when he preaches in public what he has learned from Scripture.

Various writers have composed treatises on the other 'rungs', how and when one must 'mount' them.[4] Little has been said[5] up to now about preaching: its nature, by whom and to whom it should be delivered, on what subjects and in what manner, at what time or in what place. We have thought it worthwhile to compile a treatise on the subject, for the edification of our 'neighbors'.[6]

CHAPTER I: ON PREACHING

First, then, we must see what preaching is, what form it should take—in the surface aspect of its words, and in the weight of its thoughts—and how many kinds of preaching there are. Secondly, we must consider who the preachers should be; thirdly, to whom the sermon should be delivered; fourthly, for what reasons, and fifthly, in what place.

Preaching is an open and public instruction in faith

---

4.   Manuscript variant: 'it is clear enough how and when one must mount the other steps, on which various writers . . . ' .
5.   Var.: 'few, indeed, have spoken'.
6.   Among Alan's mediaeval predecessors, we might number Guibert of Nogent, whose *Liber quo ordine sermo fieri debeat* is printed in PL 156:21-32. J. J. Murphy, in his *Bibliography of Mediaeval Rhetoric* (Toronto 1971) VI, p. 71 remarks on the absence of an early *Ars Praedicandi* tradition.

and behavior, whose purpose is the forming of men; it derives from the path of reason and from the fountainhead of the 'authorities'.[1] Preaching should be public, because it must be delivered openly. That is why Christ says: 'What I say to you in your ear, preach upon the the housetops.'* For if preaching were hidden, it would be suspect; it would seem to smell of heretical dogmas. The heretics preach secretly in their assemblies, so that they may the more easily deceive others. Preaching should be public because it must be delivered not to one, but to many; if it were given to a single man, it would not be preaching but teaching—for that is where the distinction lies between preaching, teaching, prophecy and public speaking. Preaching is that instruction which is offered to many, in public, and for their edification. Teaching is that which is given to one or to many, to add to their knowledge. Prophecy gives warning of what is to come, through the revelation of future events. Public-speaking is the admonishing of the people to maintain[3] the well-being of the community.[4] By means of what is called 'preaching'—instruction in matters of faith and behavior—two aspects of theology may be introduced: that which appeals to the reason and deals with the knowledge of spiritual matters, and the ethical, which offers teaching on the living of a good life. For preaching sometimes teaches about holy things, sometimes about conduct. This is what is

Mt 10:27

[112]

---

1.   That is, the 'authorities' of Holy Scripture and of the works of the Fathers.
2.   Cf. a similar list in Robert of Basevorn's *Ars Praedicandi,* chapter one. See J. J. Murphy *Three Rhetorical Arts* (California 1971) 120.
3.   Var.: 'strengthen'.
4.   A fundamental notion in classical rhetoric. See Cicero *De inventione* 1:1 ff.

meant by the angels ascending and descending. Preachers are the 'angels', who 'ascend' when they preach about heavenly matters, and 'descend' when they bend themselves to earthly things in speaking of behavior.

In the remainder of our definition, the ultimate reason for preaching—the benefit it brings—is implied in: 'whose purpose is the forming of men'. Because preaching must be dependent on reasoning and corroborated by authoritative texts, we have: 'it derives from the path of reason and from the fountainhead of the "authorities".'

Preaching should not contain jesting words, or childish remarks, or that melodiousness and harmony which result from the use of rhythm or metrical lines;[5] these are better fitted to delight the ear than to edify the soul. Such preaching is theatrical[6] and full of buffoonery, and in every way to be condemned. Of such preaching the prophet says: 'Your innkeepers mix water with the wine.'* Water is mingled with wine in the preaching in which childish and mocking words—what we may call 'effeminacies'— are put into the minds of the listeners. Preaching should not glitter with verbal trappings, with purple patches, nor should it be too much enervated by the use of colorless words[7]: the blessed keep to a middle way.[8] If it were too heavily-embroidered [the sermon]

Is 1:22

---

5.   On the use of rhythm and metre at this period, see D. Norberg *Introduction à l'étude de la versification latine médiévale* (Stockholm 1958).

6.   See D. Bigongiari 'Were there Theatres in the Twelfth and Thirteenth centuries?' *Romanic Review* 37 (1946) p. 212.

7.   A pun on the 'colors' of rhetoric.

8.   J. M. Miller *Readings in Mediaeval Rhetoric* (Indiana 1973) 231, n. 4 suggests that Alan may be mimicking the form of the Beatitudes here.

would seem to have been contrived with excessive care, and elaborated to win the admiration of man, rather than for the benefit of our neighbors, and so it would move less the hearts of those who heard it. Those who preach in this way are to be compared with

[113]

Mt 23:5

the pharisees, who made the tassels of their garments long, and wore large phylacteries.* Such preaching may be said to be suspect, yet it is not to be wholly condemned, but rather tolerated. For St Paul says: 'On whatever occasion Christ is preached, I rejoice

Ph 1:18

in it and shall rejoice.'* It serves no purpose to interpolate at intervals the phrase: 'to the greater glory of Christ,'[9] for Christ is no less angered by false praise than by a denial of the truth. Such—as a rule— is the teaching of heretics, who propound truths and introduce falsehoods among them.[10] It is said of them: 'even jackals bare their breasts and feed their

Lm 4:3; cf. Rv 9:7-10

young.'* These jackals have the faces of young girls, but the feet of horses. Horses' hooves are not cloven, but stand squarely on the ground. By 'jackals', there- fore, we should understand 'heretics', who have the faces of young girls, but whose bodies end in the scorpion's sting. For first they propound the truth, and then they draw false conclusions from it. They have indeed the feet of horses, for they do not divide

affectus mentis

their hearts' desire* between the love of God and the love of their neighbor, but they set all their desires on earthly pleasures. Such preaching must be wholly rejected, because it is full of vices and dangers. There should be some weight in the thought of a good sermon, so that it may move the spirits of its hearers,[11]

9.   Var.: 'the Christian religion'.
10. Var.: 'Draw false conclusions from them'.
11. Var. [add]: 'to tears'. Cf. Cicero *Orator* 21:69 and DDC 4:12:27.

stir up the mind,[12] and encourage repentance. Let the
sermon rain down doctrines, thunder forth admoni-
tions, soothe with praises, and so in every way work
for the good of our neighbors. There are some who
make earthly gain the motive for their preaching, but
their preaching is extravagant; such are rather merchants than preachers, and so their preaching is to
be heard and endured. That is why the Lord says: 'Do
what they tell you to do, but do not follow the exam-

Mt 23:3   ple they set.'*

There are three kinds of preaching: that which is
by the spoken word, of which it is said: 'Go, preach

Mk 16:15   the Gospel to every creature.'* Another is by means
of the written word, as when the Apostle says that he
has 'preached' to the Corinthians because he has

1 Co 5:9,11   written them a letter.* The third is by deed, as it is
said: 'Every work of Christ is our instruction.'[13]

This should be the form of preaching: it should
develop from, as it were, its own proper foundation,
from a theological authority—especially a text from
the Gospels, the Psalms, the Epistles of Paul, or the
Books of Solomon, for in these, in particular, edify-
ing instruction resounds. Texts should also[14] be taken
from other books of Holy Writ if necessary, and if
they have a bearing on the theme in hand.

And so the preacher must win the goodwill[15] of his

---

12.   Cf. Anselm *Proslogion,* ed. F. S. Schmitt *Anselmi Opera Omnia,*
6 vols. (Rome/Edinburgh 1938-68) 1:97, Ch. I: *Excitatio mentis ad
contemplandum deum.*
13.   Not a Scriptural quotation.
14.   Var.: 'therefore.'
15.   *Captatio benevolentiae,* the winning of goodwill, is one of the
parts of a letter in the contemporary Art of Letter-Writing; it has its
origin in classical rhetoric.

audience through the humility he shows in his own person, and through the profitableness of his subject-matter. He must say that he propounds the Word of God to his listeners so that it may bring forth fruit in their minds, not for any earthly gain, but to set them on their way and to help them make progress. He must make it clear that the sermon is not designed to arouse the foolish acclaim of the mob, nor tempered *[114]* to win popular favor, nor shaped to evoke applause, as in a theatre. It is composed to instruct the souls of the listeners, so that they may concentrate, not on who is speaking to them, but on what he is saying.[16] It is not the sharpness of the thorn that we should dwell on, but the sweetness of the rose. Honey can be sucked from the broken reed, and fire may be struck from a stone. Thus, if he is committed to his task, [the preacher] should show how profitable it is to hear the word of God.

He should also assure his listeners that he will speak briefly and to their profit, and that he has been led to speak only by his love for his listeners; that he does not speak as one greater in knowledge or in wisdom, or as one who lives a better life, but because things are sometimes revealed to the little ones which are not shown to the great; and at such a time, the great ought to be silent. And because sometimes the great do not wish to preach, it is not surprising if lesser men then prattle. For if the learned are silent, *Lk 19:40* the very stones will speak and cry out.* So the preacher should come to the exposition of the proposed text, and bend everything he says to the edification of the listener. Let him not begin with a text which is too obscure or too difficult,[17] in case his listeners are put

---

16. Var.: 'who it is who is spoken of'.
17. Cf. DDC 4:9:23.

off by it and so listen less attentively. Nor, in the expounding of his authority, should he move too quickly away from his text, in case the beginning should be out of keeping with the middle and the middle with the end.[18] He should also bring in other authorities to corroborate the first, especially those which are relevant to his subject. He may also, on occasion, insert sayings of the pagan writers—just as the Apostle Paul sometimes introduces quotations from the philosophers into his epistles, for he will make an apt point [19] if he provides a fresh illumination by such a skilful juxtaposition. He may also introduce moving words which soften hearts and encourage tears. But let the sermon be brief,[20] in case prolixity should cause boredom. When the preacher sees that his hearers' minds are moved, and that they weep freely, and that their expressions are downcast, he should hold back a little, but not too much, for, as Lucretius says: 'Nothing dries up faster than a tear.'[21] Finally, he should make use of examples[22] to prove what he says, because teaching by means of examples is a familiar method. For instance:

CHAPTER II: ON DESPISING THE WORLD

If the preacher wishes to invite his listeners to despise

---

18.   Horace, *Ars Poetica* 1:152.
19.   *elegantem locum:* the *locus,* or topic, was an important element in 'rhetorical argument' from classical times.
20.   The author of the *Rhetorica ad Herennium* advises orators to be brief in their statements of the facts: 1:9:14.
21.   Cf. Cicero *Part. Orat.* xvii:57.
22.   On *exempla,* see Introduction pp. 5–6.

Qo 1:2

the world, let him bring before them this text: 'Vanity of vanities! All is vanity!'* What authority so teaches the vanity of earthly things and the unworthiness of man as does this one? It shows that all things pass away and nothing endures. According to this authority we should distinguish three forms of worldly vanity. There is the vanity of what passes away, the vanity of worldly care, and the vanity of deceitfulness. According to the vanity of what passes away, all things are subject to change. On this topic St Paul says: 'every creature was made subject to vanity.'* The vanity of worldly care makes a man concentrate all his desire on worldly things; whence: 'The Lord knows the thoughts of men, that they are vain.'* On the same subject, Persius, writing in comic vein, says: 'How great a folly are the cares of mankind over their affairs!'* The vanity of deceitfulness is the telling of lies, of which it is said: 'Everyone speaks vain things to his neighbor.'* In such a way the preacher should substantiate from the authorities every division of the subject which he proposes, otherwise every division is uncertain and unreliable.[1] He should show where vanity is to be found in all earthly things, where there is the vanity of vanities and where all is vanity. For it is vanity if riches come to a man, for they quickly pass away; if they last, they make a man their slave and, that, you see, is the vanity of vanities. If they diminish, all is vanity.

[115]
Rm 8:20

Ps 94:11;
1 Co 3:20

Satura 1:1

Ps 12:3

In riches is the vanity of that which passes away, for they perish; the vanity of worldly care, for men concentrate all their desire on them; the vanity of deceitfulness, because men spit out lies for the sake of getting and keeping wealth. Where is there a greater vanity than in riches which, when they promise

---

1.   On *divisio* see Introduction p. 6.

happiness, take away that very thing; which promise
security but bring only fear? For where is a greater
fear to be found than among the rich, who are in
terror of everything for fear of losing their wealth?
They do not trust their children; even a wife's love is
suspect; they fear those who are greater and they live
in terror of robbers. They dream of things which do
not exist and they do not believe in what is really
there. Where is there a greater vanity than in riches,
which promise fullness and leave a man hungry?
They return drunkenness for thirst; far from satisfy-
ing greed, they increase covetousness. They do not
enrich the mind, but exhaust its resources. They are
filled with a kind of unspeakable emptiness and
empty of a kind of indescribable fullness.[2]

Where is vanity if not in worldly honors? They
show their favor to a man only so they may destroy
him. They lift him up only to cast him down. They
raise him up only to throw him the more heavily to
the ground. In these is the vanity of vanities, for there
is in honor an unbearable burden, and in the burden a
valueless honor. All is vanity in honors when they
utterly desert a man. There is vanity in the enticements of worldly things when first they give pleasure,
the vanity of vanities when they come to be loathed,
and all is vanity when we are led by them to death. At
first they soothe, then they sting, and at last they
destroy. Similarly there is a deceitfulness in venial sin,
the deceitfulness of deceitfulness in mortal sin, and in
inflexible sin all is deceitfulness. There is deceitfulness
in punishment, the deceitfulness of deceitfulness in
error, and in hell, all is deceitfulness. Therefore, ab-
horring vanity and fearing deceitfulness, let us run our
course towards the highest truth, that is, to God in

/116/

2.   Cf. Misc. 16; *Textes* p. 278.

whom is the Truth of Truths, through the fulfilling of
his promises. In him is all truth, for he himself is all in
all that is holy.*

1 Co 12:6

When he has thus shown that the world is to be
despised because of the nature of temporal things, the
preacher should demonstrate the same theme from its
ultimate principle. This consists in two things: that is,
in doing what is profitable and in avoiding what is
unprofitable. Contempt for the world through doing
what is profitable may be urged in this way: 'O man,
if you will despise the world, you will have God, the
Creator of the world and its Lord, for your reward.'
Contempt for the world through the avoidance of
what is unprofitable can be urged like this: 'O man,
if you will despise the world and what is vain, fear will
not cause you to tremble, hope will not desert you,
sadness will not constrain you, nor will your joy fade.
You will be no one's slave; you will be free; you will
not fear the blows of any adversary. Your conscience
will be at peace, and you will await the coming of
death with a quiet mind. Death will be welcome and
after death there will be the hope of blessedness. If,
however, you cling to the pleasures of this world,
your conscience, entangled in earthly vanities, will
be torn, and death hateful; after death your end will
be eternal punishment. What will you feel then? In
death, devils will appear to you, horrible adversaries,
waiting to carry off your soul to hell. And you will
find that those things which were pleasing to you in
life will be savage in death. Where will your pleasure be
then? Where will your earthly friends be then? Where
will the delights of this world be then? After riches
comes eternal poverty, after honors degradation, and
for pleasures you exchange eternal bitterness.'

After this, let the preacher conclude his admonition
with instructive examples, showing how the Fathers

of old despised the world and yet the world
flourished in their day, while it shrivelled up in
their hearts. Now, when the world is shrivelling up
in itself, it should not flourish in our hearts, but we
should put it to flight by fleeing it, leave it to its sliding, lest we slip with its sliding or rush with it to
our ruin.

CHAPTER III: ON DESPISING ONESELF

If the preacher sets out to encourage his listeners to
despise themselves, let him use this text: 'Children,
remember your final end and you will never sin.'* Or
this: 'I am a worm and not a man.'* Or this: 'Man
who is born of woman is filled with many sorrows,'*
or some similar text by means of which human
wretchedness may be expressed. He should then go
on in this way: Remember your final end and that of
the world; remember the Day of Judgement. Consider
your own end, remembering that you were conceived
in sin and born in pain; your life is a punishment, and
death an inevitability, that life is disappearing or
promises to disappear, while death is at hand or
threatens to be. In what then shall a man glory? Conceived in sin, born in pain, his life is full of effort; he
must certainly die. O man, remember that you were a
seed in fluid, that you are a channel for dung, and
that you will be food for worms.* After your death a
worm is born from your tongue: this denotes the sin
of loose speech. From your stomach come lice, which
represent the sin of gluttony, from your spine a scorpion, which signifies the sin of dissipation, from your
head a toad, which means the sin of pride.
O man, you are a worm born from the earth. You

Si 7:40
Ps 22:7
Jb 14:1

[117]

Cf. Misc. *11*

are a worm while you live, because you are earth-bound; you are a worm when you die, for you will be given to the worms for food. Remember, O man, that because you are earth you will return to the earth, and because you are ashes you will return to ashes.

*Cf. Gn 3:19, 18: 27, Jb 34:15, Si 17:31

Because you are dust, you will return to dust.* On your behalf, Job said: 'I have said to corruption, "you are my father", and to the worms, "you are my

†Jb 17:14

mother and my sister!" '† O man, remember the final end of your beauty, how 'all flesh is like grass and all

Is 40:6

its glory like that of the flower of the field.'* For 'Beauty is a frail blessing, and as the years pass it grows

Ovid, Ars ama-toria 2:113

less; it is diminished with its own span of life.'* Remember how beauty is lost in death, how the prick of a single pin destroys it, how sickness damages it and how it is ruined by old age. If you boast of your strength, remember to what your strength will come at last, how old age weakens it, sickness drains it, and death wholly destroys it. If you brag of your wisdom, hear what the Lord says through Isaiah: 'I will destroy the wisdom of the wise and bring to nothing the

Is 29:14; 1 Co 1:19
*1 Co 3:19
†1 Co 8:1

understanding of the learned.'* And elsewhere: 'The wisdom of this world rates as foolishness before God.'* Consider how 'Learning puffs up, while love edifies',† how the philosophers 'through the medium of created things had some perception of the invisible things of God, but because they went astray in their reasoning their misguided minds were given up to

Rm 1:20

error.'* If you boast of your birth, remember the final end of every nation, and how 'Every race of men arose from a like beginning'.[1] Since for all men there is one beginning in birth and one ending in death, to achieve nobility is better than to be born noble; for while the latter is more common, the former is a finer

---

1.   Boethius *De consolatione Philosophiae* III metr. vi:1.

thing. The royal purple, too, comes under the rule of
death, since death overthrows both the palaces of
kings and the hovels of poor men. If you boast of
riches and earthly pleasures, consider how they are
rather enemies than friends. You should not feel
secure in them, but rather timid and uncertain. Think
how you came naked from your mother's womb and

Jb 1:21   how, naked, you will return.*

Learn to open the house your mother made to
poverty, to bind your pleasures under the yoke of
reason. Learn that there is shallow satisfaction in the
enjoyment of earthly goods. The ruddy color[2] of
metals of little value gleams on the surface. The most

[118]   precious metals are those which lie in a deep vein, and
which will yield ever more richly to digging. To these
heavenly treasures direct your mind, so that where
your treasure is, there may your heart be also: 'Do
not lay up for yourself treasure upon earth, where
thieves break in and steal, but lay up for yourself
treasures in heaven, which neither moth nor rust will

Mt 6:21   destroy.'* For, as Seneca says: 'These things in which
the common mob takes delight give a slight and superficial pleasure. They lack at root the deep joys of
life.'[3] Learn, then, to despise those things which have
a merely superficial glory, and which are lent you by
someone else, which are not for you. Strive to reach
the true good and to take pleasure in what is proper
to you.

Do not glory in fine clothing. What glory is there
in the fleeces of sheep and in the castings of worms?
What is the good of making the filth of the body fine,

---

2.   Var.: *utilitas:* value.
3.   Cf. Seneca, *Letter* 23:5. On this and Alan's other 'Seneca'
quotations, see J. E. B. Mayor 'Seneca in Alan of Lille' *The Journal of
Philology* 20 (1892) 1-6.

of adorning the dung-pit of the flesh? Remember
then your final end, which is written in the book
of knowledge. You may read about yourself in the
book of experience. You may discover yourself in
the book of conscience.[4] The book of knowledge—
written in a volume—may reprehend you, as well as
the book of experience written in the heart. You read
in the book of knowledge: 'Know yourself'. In the
book of experience you will read that the flesh battles
Ga 5:17   against the spirit,* in the book of conscience that
'The day of judgement circles on remorseless wings'.[5]

O man, look at yourself in this threefold mirror,
and you will not be pleased by the sight of yourself.
The glass in which you should behold yourself is
triple: the mirror of Scripture, the mirror of nature,
and the mirror of creation. In the mirror of Scripture
you will read of your condition. In the mirror of
creation you will behold your wretchedness. In the
mirror of nature you will see that you stand accused.

But in your own nature, a threefold mirror reflects
back again: the glass of reason, the glass of the senses,
and the glass of the flesh. As the philosopher says,[6]
there is a certain kind of mirror in which the left
appears on the left and the right on the right. This
mirror is that of reason,[7] which tells us to seek the
'right', that is, the things of heaven, and to flee the
'left', that is, the things of earth. There is another
kind of mirror, in which the right-hand side appears
to be on the left, and the left on the right. This is
the glass of the senses, which tells us that the things of

---

4.   On 'the book of experience' etc., cf. Misc 9 and 11. Cf. Bernard
Conv 3 (SBOp 4:73).
5.   Statius, *Thebaid* 1:51; Cf. Misc. 11.
6.   Seneca, *Quaestiones naturales* 1:5:14 and 1:5-1:7 *passim*,
Cf. Lucretius, *De rerum natura* 4:250-320.
7.   Var.: "the 'right' in this mirror is reason . . . . "

earth are to be sought after, and the things of heaven
are to be put from us. There is yet another kind of
glass in which the face appears upside-down. This is
the glass of the flesh which turns all human nature
upside-down.

Look at yourself, then, in the mirror of reason,
that you may follow its instructions. Look at yourself
in the mirror of the senses, to bring them under the
control of reason. Look at yourself in the mirror of
the flesh, that you may defeat carnal lusts. Set yourself before three mirrors: first the mirror of providence, so that you may beware of the dangers which
threaten you; secondly, before the glass of circumspection, that you may avoid the opposing vice. Hold
to a middle way. You will walk most safely in the
middle, for nature, too, is the friend of moderation.
Thirdly, look in the glass of wariness, in case a vice is
hiding itself under the guise of a virtue, for often
cruelty pretends to be justice and is in fact the absence of mercy. And so, through this threefold mirror,
/119/   you will come to the threefold vision of a clear conscience, divine contemplation and eternal life.

CHAPTER IV: AGAINST GLUTTONY

If the preacher wishes to encourage his listeners to
avoid gluttony, he can use this text: 'I treat my body
1 Co 9:27   harshly and make it obey me.'* Again: 'Let us live
Tt 2:12   soberly and righteously and piously in this world.'*
I say that the body must be treated harshly so that it
may serve us. Take care of it, but do not be its slave,
for he who is a slave to the body is a slave to many
things; he fears too much for it, who sets his all upon
it. Honor is cheap to him whose body is too dear to

Seneca, Ep 14.2   him.* The Lord says in the Gospel: 'See that your
hearts are not overcharged with surfeiting and drunk-
Lk 21:34   enness and the cares of this life.'* Paul, too, says: 'Do
Eph 5:18   not be drunk with wine, in which is dissipation.'* Solomon says: 'Wine is full of dissipation and drunkenness
causes riotousness. He who delights in these things
Pr 20:1   is unwise.'* Jesus, Son of Sirach, remarks: 'A drunken
laborer will not grow rich. Wine and women cause
Si 19:12   wise men to go astray and make them imprudent.'*
'A little wine is sufficient for a wise man and for a
learned man. You will not be troubled by it in your
sleep, nor will you feel your labors. Wine taken in
Si 31:22   moderation brings health to both body and mind.'*
Isidore says: 'Wherever satiety and drunkenness are
found, there lust will govern.'[1] Behave then, O man,
in such a way that you do not appear to live for the
sake of your body; conduct yourself as though you
were able to live without a body and—as far as you
can—rather believe the flesh to be a necessary thing
than an important one.

From the body are born as a matter of course
pleasures which are brief, reprehensible, and, unless
they are controlled, immoderate, and liable to turn
into the very opposite of pleasure. Therefore discipline the body, which is like a dog or a slave or a
beast of burden. The more a slave is indulged, the
more likely he is to become an idle wastrel. The
more a dog is beaten, the more it barks. The better a
beast of burden is cared for, the more it kicks its
master. Then how zealously is gluttony to be avoided
which, when it makes its home in the body, reduces
this vessel of the mind and spirit to a dung-heap and
turns our flesh to filth. It bends the spirit, which

---

1.   The thought, but not the words, are to be found in *Sent.* 2:4;
PL 83:648.

is the true school of the virtues, the governor of reason, the temple of the Lord and the foundation of
immortality, and inclines it towards a parading of
vices, the filthiness of crime, the grime of sin, the
display of uncleanness. This is gluttony, for whose
sake you immerse yourself in business, and labor in
castles. You do service to the rich and you put up
with their pride. You flatter them and you speak to
them placatingly. Therefore avoid gluttony. Do not
be a slave to the flesh, but take care of it. Sustain it,
do not cosset it. Rule it; do not rouse it.

    O man, do you know what gluttony is? Gluttony
is the tomb of the mind, a heap of dung, the source of
[120]   dissipation, the mother of nausea. Your stomach is
fortified against gluttony if it can say: O man, I ask
for what I need, but I will not take more than I need.
Do not burden me, but give me the food I require.
I ask what nature demands, what necessity asks.
What is more than that is of the Devil, for: 'Food and
water are sufficient for the people.'[2] O man, why take
trouble to add to dung and fill the dung-pit? Consider
your nature; understand the measure of your stomach.
You know where weaknesses of the body come from,
and loss of reason—it is certainly from a great weight
of food, from a stream of liquid, or rather, a flood!
Whence comes fever if not from gluttony? Why does a
man fall into a fit, if not because he is drunk? Surely
paralysis comes from drunkenness and dropsy from
wine-bibbing? What is drunkenness but a madness, a
robber of virtue, an image of death, the likeness of a
madman? When he is drunk, a man swells with haughty
pride, is brutal to his servant and vicious to his enemy.
Drunkenness confuses his words, clouds his eyes,
makes him walk unsteadily, tortures his stomach,

---

2.   Lucan, *Pharsalia* 4:381.

distends his intestines, makes his head dizzy. It drives
out the very sense of shame from the mind, and takes
the guard from a man's tongue. It takes away modesty
and breaks the seal of chastity.

It is drunkenness which brings any hidden evil out
into the open when too much wine has taken possession of the mind. Just as new wine fermenting bursts
the wine-jar, and what is in the wine comes foaming
to the top, so when a man is drowned in drunkenness,
the secret which lies in his mind comes up from the
depths of his heart to his mouth. Just as the wine spills
out from the bodily stomach to the mouth, so from
the stomach of the mind, the secret comes forth in
words. Just as a drunken man cannot hold his wine, so
he vomits forth his secret.

This is one of the daughters of idolatry, to whom
the stomach is God.* She worships Bacchus. To coin
a name, she may be called a 'Bacchus-worshipper'. He
is idolator enough who puts his stomach before God,
devotes himself more to Bacchus than to God, grows
disgusting in his drunkenness and wallows like a beast
in its dung.

Ph 3:19

O man, consider the rich man who feasted splendidly every day. Consider, on the other hand, Lazarus,
who lay outside his door, covered in sores. The rich
man enjoyed his good living, and so he was cast into
hell. In life he feasted splendidly. After death, he
thirsted for a drop of water. First he was clothed in
purple and afterwards he was surrounded by the flames
of hell. In life, Lazarus was a beggar. After death, he lay
in the bosom of Abraham. Here, he was a poor man;
there, he is rich. Here, he was full of sores; there, he is
comforted by the hope of blessedness.* Consider, man,
how through gluttony, Adam lost paradise;† Elijah,
through abstinence, went up to heaven.* Noah uncovered his nakedness because of overindulgence in
wine.* Moses, through abstinence, was found worthy

[121]
*Lk 16:19-31
†Gn 3:13

*2 K 2:1

*Gn 9:21

Ex 19-20
Gn 19:32-7
2 S 24; 1 Ch 21

to speak with God.* Lot fell into dishonor through
drunkenness.* David, through abstinence, made the
reparation of penance.*

O man, learn from nature. She teaches you what
should be the rule for living. The law of nature is that
you should dispel hunger and thirst, and to do this it
is not necessary that you should go far across the sea,
nor that you should voyage in ships. What nature
requires is easily prepared and ready to hand.[3] Take
up arms, then, against gluttony, and fortify yourself
against drunkenness. Take the remedy of fasting
against the threat of such a sickness. Abstain from
food, lest the flesh be sportive. Fast from worldly
pleasure, lest the mind grow lazy, and from sin, lest
the spirit grow languid. We should beat our 'beast',
that is our flesh, with this threefold fasting, so that it
may not raise its hoof to kick us. Our 'beast' must be
corrected by means of the stick, spurs, bridle, and
goad. For if our flesh wishes to wander into forbidden
places, it must be prevented by the discipline of the
bridle. It must be chastised with fastings as if with
spurs. It must be castigated with vigils, as if with
sticks. It must be brought to its senses by the goad
of fear.

CHAPTER V: AGAINST DISSIPATION

If the preacher wishes to encourage his listeners to
avoid dissipation, he can begin with this text: 'Avoid
fornication'.* The Lord says in the Gospel: 'Have
your loins girded, and have lamps burning in your
hands'.* Paul says: 'God will judge fornicators and
adulterers'.* Solomon tells us: 'A harlot is like a deep

1 Co 6:18

Lk 12:35
Heb 13:4

---

3.   This passage is expanded in some manuscripts without adding to
the argument.

pit; she lies in wait along the road like a robber, and
destroys those whom she sees, if they are not wary'.*
Jesus, Son of Sirach, says: 'Do not give a woman
power over your soul, lest she make assaults on your
virtue and you are overthrown'.* Jerome says: 'Woe
to him whose dissipation is brought to an end only by
death. For chastity may be preserved among the rich
only with difficulty. A lovely outward appearance
betrays a soul befouled, and lust is lord in silken garments'.[1] He who indulges in lust is dead while he
lives, and he who is drunk is dead and buried. Gregory
says: 'While the stomach is distended with fullness, the
sting of lust stirs'.[2] He who bridles the pleasure of his
lustful thoughts does not slip into consenting to lust.
If pleasure in fornication delights his mind more than
the love of chastity, sin still rules the man. All uncleanness and unchastity is called fornication. It is better to
die than to indulge in fornication. It is better to die
than to be besmirched by lust. Desire thrusts a man
down into hell. Lust burns more fiercely in someone
who has plenty of leisure. When you are young,
come close to a raging fire more readily than to a
young woman. When physical horrors are to be fled
and feared, how much more are spiritual monsters to
be fled and put to flight! What monster is more terri-
ble than dissipation, which bears the face of a young girl
and the image of desire, but its body is a she-goat of
stinking lust, its tail a wolf, that snatcher-away of
virtue?

This is that vice which has a close likeness with hell.
In hell there are three things: a foetid smell, the burning of the worm of conscience, and a devouring flame.
So dissipation stinks in its infamy, scorches the conscience, and devours a man with desire. This is the
vice more damnable than any horror. It empties the
purse, enervates the body, intoxicates the mind,

Pr 23:27-8

Si 9:2

[122]

---

1.   *Ep* 117:6, cf. Ps-Aug. *Hom. ad Monachos* PL 30:315A.
2.   Cf. *Moralia in Job* xxxi:xlv; PL 76:622A.

emasculates a man's thinking, besmirches the spirit.
It destroys a man's reputation, offends his neighbor,
and separates him from God.

This is the vice whose pleasure is soon past and
whose pain lasts for ever. The desire for it causes
anxiety and folly; the act itself is an abomination
and full of ignominy; its result is punishment and
shame. In that vice these three things are loathsome:
the burning eagerness to achieve what is desired; the
effort involved in carrying it out; and the stench of
its completion. Behold what vileness! What a satis-
fying of desire in dung-pits! You will appease a hunger and enjoy a pleasure which carries a grave punishment. Its pleasure lasts for a moment; its bitterness is
everlasting.

This is the vice which hates the light, seeks darkness and a covering, and sets a guard at the door. This
is the fly which turns sweet oil rancid, which is born
from the dung-pit and which dwells in filth. The
place where it settles is infected. This is dissipation,
which is the daughter of gluttony, a stench born of
the dung-pit of the flesh, a smell begotten of the filth
of the body. It feeds on uncleanness and delights in
the flesh. Chastity is an ointment in which there are,
so to speak, different kinds of 'fragrance': purity of
mind, cleanliness of body, restraint of gesture,
modesty in dress, abstinence in eating, reticence in
speaking. Dissipation turns this oil rancid, because it
defiles the mind, besmirches the body, makes gestures
bold, dress womanish, meals excessive, words
unguarded; and so lust with its arms lays siege to
chastity. These arms are: appearance and address,
touch and kiss and deed. When first dissipation tempts
a man to desire through what he sees, it attacks his
chastity; secondly by addressing him, it does injury
to his chastity; thirdly it spits in the face of shame

with a kiss; fourthly it shakes modesty by a touch; fifthly it kills it in the deed itself. Battle with lust must be engaged in the Parthian way. Just as the Parthians when fleeing put the enemy into disorder and when retreating overcame them, so lust is to be put to flight by fleeing and slain by retreating.*

Cf. Horace, Odes
1:19:11, 2:13:17

This is that vice which entwines the three things which may drive a man from his home, that is, smoke, a flood, and his wife. The wife is carnal lust, the smoke the great cloud of ill-repute, the flood the flood of desire. These three keep the spirit from peace of heart, from serenity of mind, from tranquillity of heart. O man, read in examples what the vice of dissipation brings with it, so that the deeds of others may be your instruction. Through lust, David fell into murder.* Because of dissipation, Ammon suffered the sword of Absalom.* Daniel, through chastity, deserved to be given the power to interpret dreams;* Joseph, through chastity, merited the first office in Egypt.* Jezebel, for her evil deed, earned ruin and death;* the Blessed Virgin, through her virginity, deserved to become the Mother of God.*

[123]

2 S 11:16
2 S 13:28
Dn 7:11

Gn 41:41
1 K 21:23
Lk 1:35

Do you wish to avoid lust? Beware of gluttony, which foments lust; it is the beginning of dissipation and the bridge to shamelessness, the prelude to incontinence. O man, it is lust which makes the imagination sluggish, the senses dull, the understanding dim. Further, to put it even more strongly, it turns a man into a beast; it even degrades a man below the level of a beast, for the cattle observe the proper times for their lust, but you are lustful all the time. The beast follows nature; you debauch yourself. The beast confines himself to one of his own kind; you dissipate yourself among many.

CHAPTER VI: AGAINST AVARICE

If the preacher wishes to incline the hearts of his listeners against covetousness and greed, let him take the theme of his sermon from that authority which declares avarice to be the service of idols,* or from that which says: 'There are three things which are never satisfied, and even a fourth which never says, "enough".'* For 'The more they drink, the more they thirst'.* No vice is more likely to lead to sin, when it burns with the thirst for gain: 'O cursed lust for gold, to what do you not drive mortal hearts?'*

Whereas other things are held within firm bounds, avarice has no limit. The earth is bounded by its limits; water is held in by its banks; the air has its boundaries and the sky is contained by its borders. Only avarice is not checked by measure. O man, many things take up arms against you on account of avarice; many things complain against you: fortune, nature, your own flesh, charity, your neighbor, the world and God.

Hear what Fortune says against you. 'O man, why do you seek to be a member of my household? Why do you ask for my favor? If I give you riches, it is only to take them away; I give the more generously so that I may have more to snatch away; I give the more generously, so that I may torture you the more fiercely. I make myself appear serene, so that the thunderclap, when it comes, may be the more frightening. You who are in safety, why do you look to me for trouble? You who are on level ground, why do you yearn for my precipice? You who are in harbor, why do you pant for my shipwreck?

Cf. Eph 5:5

Pr 30:15
Ovid, Fasti *1:216*

Virgil, Aeneid *3:56*

[124]

Hear what nature says against you! 'O man, I begot
you without honors, so that you may return without
honors. I bore you without wealth, so that you
should come to me again in poverty. You entered on
this life without earthly glory, and without earthly
glory you shall leave it. O man, do you seek to do
something which is foreign to you? Certainly, those
things with which you were not born are foreign to
you, and those things which cannot be with you
for ever—nor even for very long—deny themselves
yours. Consider this saying of the philosopher: 'Poverty with joy is an honorable thing'.[1] With joy, there
is no such thing as poverty. The man who welcomes
poverty is rich. The poor man is not he who has little,
but he who desires more. If you live according to
nature, you will never be poor. If you live according
to your expectations, you will never be rich. Nature
desires very little, and expectation a great deal. Natural desires are finite, but those born of false expectations know no bounds, for there is no end to false
expectation. Draw back, then, from vain things, and
when you wish to know whether your desires are
natural ones, or blind desires, consider whether they
can be quickly satisfied. If, after a long struggle to
attain your desire, you find that something further
always remains out of reach, you will know that that
desire is not born of nature. O how much to be desired
is honest poverty! Riches stand in the way of many
good deeds. Poverty is quickly satisfied and has no
cares. If you wish to serve God it befits you either to
be poor or to behave as if you were poor.'

Hear, O man, what your own flesh says against
you! 'Why do you complain against me? What quarrel
have you with me? You call me the touchwood which

---

1.   Seneca *Ad Lucil. Ep.* 2:6

sparks sin, a savage tyrant over your members, the weakness of nature and the devil's goad. Why do you impute to me the fact that you are afflicted with greed and bloated with desire? I could lay more accusations against you, bring more arguments to bear, since without a spark I lie inert and without a stimulus I am idle. It is you who awaken me to desire and excite me to avarice. You give me the arms with which to fight against you; you incite me to be wild and encourage me to violence.'

Hear what charity says against you! 'O man, why do you make yourself wealthy with things of which your neighbor stands in need? Why do you keep for yourself things which should be given to the poor? Why do you feed moths and worms with things which should go to sustain the poor? Do you wish to be the best of merchants, an outstanding moneylender, a wise steward? Give what you cannot keep, that you may obtain those things which cannot be taken from you; give a little, that you may receive an hundredfold. Give away those possessions which are not properly yours, so that you may obtain an everlasting inheritance.'

Hear what your neighbor says against you! 'O man, why do you injure me? Why do you grind me to death for what is mine? Why do you cheat with lies and plan to commit crimes, to empty my purse and cheat me of my money? If you injure me, recompense will be required of you at once. If you rob me of my money, you will have robbed yourself of your soul. If you wound me in my body, you will first have wounded yourself in your mind.'

Hear what the elements say against you, and *[125]* especially the earth, your mother: 'Why do you do injury to your mother? Why do you do violence to me who brought you forth from my womb? Why

Cf. Ps 129:2 do you disturb me with the plough,* so that I may
return your investment in seed an hundredfold? Why
do you dig into me, your mother, to make me give up
my gold? Are those things not sufficient which I give
you abundantly and of my own free will, that you
should tear things from me by force? Let the time
come when you will return whence you came, when
I shall receive you and enfold you in my bosom; then
I shall expose you to beetles as you exposed me to
blows!'

Hear what the sea says against you: 'O man, why
do your ships make troughs in me? Why do you beat
me with oars and tear at my depths with nets? Is it
surprising that I drown you, that I attack you with
storms and all kinds of blows?'

Hear what the Lord says against you: 'Why is it,
man, that you set the creature before the Creator?
To him you prefer a coin, a creation of God; you prefer the earth to the heavens, the mire to the sky, the
transitory to the eternal. Consider how I have formed
you from the dust and made you in my own image.
Remember that my hands have made you, and
moulded every part of you. Are you grateful to men
for money and ungrateful to me for your very life? If
you are not grateful for what has been given you in
the past, be grateful for what is given you now, so
that even if what I have already given cannot move
you, my promises may do so. If the hope of everlasting life cannot persuade you, let the fear of hell do
so.'

Thus warned, let man avoid avarice and not set his
heart on riches, for authority says: 'It is as difficult
for a camel to pass through the eye of a needle as for
a man who puts his trust in riches to enter the King-
Mt 19:24 dom of God'.* Paul, too, says: 'The love of money
1 Tm 6:10 is the root of every evil'.* Greed brings no profit to

the man filled with greed. Avarice and the love of
money is worse than any sin. Hence the Lord says in
Lk 12:15   the Gospel: 'Beware of all covetousness',* and Paul:
'No fornicator, no unclean or avaricious man has an
Eph 5:5   inheritance in the Kingdom of God'.* Solomon, too:
Qo 5:9   'The covetous man is not to be satisfied with money'.*
And: 'He who loves riches does not enjoy the benefits
Ibid.   they bring'.* On the same subject Cyprian says: 'The
covetous man is like hell itself'.[2] Someone else
remarks: 'The covetous man "lacks" what he has just
as much as what he does not have.'[3] O brothers, if you
renounce your desires, you leave behind you many
encumbrances. For God asks for your heart, and does
not value your sweat for gain.

CHAPTER VII: AGAINST SLOTH

If the preacher wishes to arm a man against sloth,
let him use these authorities: 'The slothful beast will
Si 22:2   be pelted with dung'.* Again: 'Arise, you who sleep,
Eph 5:14   and Christ will give you light'.* Again: 'You who lie
[126]   in the tomb, arise and hurry to the Judgement of the
Source unknown.   Saviour'.* For Seneca says: 'What is done negligently
Cf. Eph 5:14   is the most costly in the end'.† From this point, the
†Ep 1:1   preacher may proceed thus:
Dearly-beloved brethren, see how Scripture arms
us against sloth and laziness. It is sloth which draws

2.   Ps–Augustine, *De salutaribus documentis;* PL 40:1047-78.
3.   Jerome, *Ep.* 53:11, quoting *antiquuus.* The passage is found first
in Publilius Syrus, *Sententiae* 486, quoted by Seneca in *Controversiae*
7:3:8, by Quintilian *Institutio Oratoria* 8:5:6, and 9:3:64. There is a
close paraphrase in Jerome, *Ep.* 100:15.

back the Christian's hand from the plough; which

Gn 19:26
Gn 19:19
Rt 1:16

looks with Lot's wife back at Sodom;* which like
Lot fears to climb the mountain;* which like Ruth
does not want to return to Bethlehem.*

This is the sloth which makes the monk's vows
grow cool, through which he comes to dislike the
rigor of the cloister. It is sloth which desires more
delicate foods at meals, which wishes to lie on softer
beds and to be less often present at vigils. It is willing
to keep silence only for a short time, or not at all. It
is sloth which is reluctant to tackle a great task, and
grows weary of a task it has begun. Everything is bur-
densome and difficult to sloth, and nothing is easy.
It is this which dampens the zeal of the clerk, drives
the cloistered monk from his cloister, nourishes vices
and banishes virtues.

Sloth gives rise to dissipation, encourages gluttony,
sows the seeds of evil-speaking and gives rise to
quarrels. For this reason the poet says: 'Does Aegis-
thus inquire why he was made an adulterer? The

Ovid, De remedio
amoris *161*
†*Eph 5:14*

reason is clear: he was lazy!'* To such a sluggard, it is
said: 'Arise, you who sleep'.† The idle man sleeps, I
tell you, with the eyes of his mind closed. He neither
directs his understanding towards what is good nor
opens the eye of his mind to see what is necessary.
Instead, he lies in a mental stupor and dreams of
phantoms, while he gives his attention to earthly
desires.

Eph 5:14

There are three kinds of dream.*[1] The first and
most important is that of contemplation, in which a
man is granted a vision of heavenly things. The second
is that of the imagination, through which he pictures to
himself visible things. The third is that of idleness, in

---

1.   Macrobius distinguishes five kinds of dream: *Commentarium in
Somnio Scipionis* 1:3:10.

Gn 2:21
1 K 3:11-5

Eph 5:14

which a man dreams of foolish things. Of the first it is said: 'God sent sleep upon Adam'.* Of the second that: 'in his sleep, the Lord gave wisdom to Solomon'.* Of the third it is said against the idle man: 'Arise, you who sleep'.* In the first kind of dream, a man becomes like God; in the second a spirit; in the third, he becomes a beast. In the first appears God; in the second, a spirit; in the third, the devil. In the first dream the eye beholds visions; in the second, material things; in the third, the eye of reason is seduced.[2] In such a sleep, Isboseth lay in a stupor in the middle of the

2 S 4:5-7

day.* When the doorkeeper was asleep, the leaders of the robbers came in and threatened to take his life. The sleeping Isboseth is the soul drowned in the sleep of idleness. The leader of the robbers who come in to kill him are devils. While the door of a man's mind is less carefully guarded by the prudence of reason, the devil cunningly enters by that gate to slay his soul.

[127]

This sleep of idleness is brought on by a murmur, or by a shade, a light breeze or by too much weariness. Just as physical sleep is brought on by a soothing song, the gentle murmur of a fountain, or a soft breeze, so, at the prompting of a sense of well-being, the mind is led into the sleep of idleness as if by the breath of a light breeze or the murmur of bodily pleasure. The cloud of ignorance, too, brings about this sleep, and a weariness of doing honest labor also produces it. The Scriptures cry to such a sleeper: 'Arise, you who

Eph 5:14

sleep'.* Arise, I say, by the prudence of your reason, by despising evil, by doing good, and 'Christ will give

Ibid.

you light'.* For night departs, and day is at hand.

You, then, lie in the tomb of negligence, which is

---

2.   In certain manuscripts there is additional material along the same lines; some of it is included here.

whitewashed outside with the semblance of
righteousness, but inside it stinks with the idleness
of your mind, and is full of a multitude of evil
thoughts which have turned into worms. Arise from
earth to sky, turn from idleness to activity, from
dangerous sloth to the business of virtue, and hasten
to the Judgement of the Saviour. Hear what Scripture
Si 22:2   says: 'The lazy ox will be pelted with dung'.* The ox
is he who labors on the threshing-floor of the Lord.
He takes hold of Scripture in its spiritual sense, as if
by his teeth; he draws spiritual understanding from
Scripture and swallows it, as if into his stomach, for
the edification of his mind. From this spiritual food,
the superficial, literal sense is cast out like dung,
together with whatever has some taste of heresy, as
well as whatever kills by idleness the man who grows
lazy in his efforts to understand Scripture.

O man, why is it that in their deputed offices
other creatures carry out their tasks? The sun completes its annual journey, the moon runs on its
monthly round of change, and the other stars fulfil
the duties allotted to them. Brute animals are not
idle in carrying out their natural tasks. You alone,
sleepy with idleness, drift away from your duty and
make hideous the image of God in yourself. You die
while you live, and you live in death.

At least let the industry of the least and humblest
animal move you to shame—that is, the prudence of
the ant. With great foresight, he collects grain in the
summer, on which he may live when winter's famine
comes. So, in this life you must gather the fruit of good
deeds, that when winter comes—that is, the Day of
Judgement—you may have the fruit of good deeds to
support you in eternity.

Behold then the danger of slothfulness! For a long
time David was engaged in wars, and dissipation had

no hold on him. But afterwards, when he rested in
his palace, he committed adultery.* During Samson's
long battle with the Philistines, he was not captured
by his enemies, but when he slept in the bosom of
Delilah he was blinded by his foe.* Solomon did not
feel the temptation of dissipation while he worked at
the building of the Temple, but, released from his
labor, he felt the assault of lustful desires.*

This is the idleness which delivers a man unarmed
into the hands of the devil, exposes him naked to the
suggestion of evil doing and, weak, to temptation.
This deprives a man of spiritual benefits—the garment
of the virtues. It calls Satan to do battle, the flesh to
lust, the mouth to greed, the mind to neglectfulness.
Therefore be occupied with honest labor, that you
may redeem in the future what you have lost in the
past. Make use of every hour; turn every moment
to profit, that at least you may offer God the last
remains of old age, although you gave the devil the
flower of your youth. At least in old age, you may be
the soldier of Christ, although when you were young
you were the slave of the devil.

2 S 11:14

Jg 16:21
[128]

1 K 11:1

CHAPTER VIII: AGAINST ENVY

The preacher can fortify his listeners against envy
with these texts. The Lord says in the Gospel: 'Do not
envy one another',* and Peter says: 'Putting away all
malice and deceitfulness and hypocrisies and evil-
speaking and envy'.* Solomon says: 'A sound heart is
the life of the body, but envy is a rottenness of the
bones'.* Augustine, too, says: 'Envy devours all the
virtues. He is certainly a jealous man whose envy
allows a stranger's good to be his own tor-

Mt 24:10. Cf.
Ga 5:26

1 P 2:1

Pr 14:30

ment.'[1] On the same subject, Isidore says: 'What
brings benefit to a good man causes a bad or envious
man to pine away with envy'.[2] Another authority
says on the same subject: 'The envy of Satan brought
death into the world'.* Again, the poet says: 'There is
no cause for laughter like the sight of someone else's
grief'.* And: 'Tyrants have not discovered a greater
torment than the envy of the Sicilians'.†

According to these texts, the preacher may proceed
thus: You have heard, dearly beloved brothers, in
what way Holy Scripture speaks of the sin of envy,
how the evil of jealousy is reproved. For this reason,
the vice of envy is to be assiduously avoided. From
the first it vexes itself and infects its possessor, who
wounds himself before he hurts another. His own
thrusts are turned back on himself. This vice grieves
at the prosperity of others and is sad at their joy; it
rejoices in the adversity of others. O vice more to be
despised than every other vice, more disgusting than
every plague! Virtue troubles it, happiness clouds it,
blessedness upsets it and joy crucifies it!

Other vices may bring a certain brief pleasure, a
shadow of joy, an appearance of happiness. This vice
is a torment without relief, a sickness without remedy,
a labor without rest, a punishment without inter-
mission. This is the sin which is its own punishment
and does not leave itself unpunished. It besmirches
and crucifies at once; at the same time it punishes
and spoils. This is the worm born from manna; this is
the worm which shrivelled up the gourd of Jonah.*
This is the fiery serpent by which the children of

Ws 2:24

*Ovid, Metamor-
phoses 2:778*

†*Horace, Ep
I.ii.5-8*

[129]

Jon 4:7

---

1.   Cf. Ps–Augustine *Ad fratres in eremo, Sermo* xviii; PL 40:1264-6;
see J. P. Bonnes 'Un de plus grands prédicateurs du xiie siècle: Geoffroy
Louroux dit Geoffroy Babion' *R.Ben* 56 (1945/6) 177.
2.   Cf. Otloh of St Emmeram, PL 146:336B.

Nb 21:6

Israel were stung.* This is the locust which consumes the fruits of the earth.

We read how manna from heaven was given to the children of Israel. If they kept it, many worms came

Ex 16:20

forth from it.* So heavenly grace is given to the faithful and gives occasion for envy to be born in the heart of a proud man. The more the faithful man is strengthened by the manna of heavenly grace, the more the mind of the proud man is infected with envy. We read that the worm was born of the gourd under whose shelter Jonah was protected from the heat of the sun. It utterly destroyed the gourd. So envy, born like a worm from the beauty of virtue, utterly destroys the purity of conscience with which a man ought to defend himself against the attacks of the vices. And the head of Jonah—that is, the mind of man—is exposed to the fierce heat of the vices.

We read how the sons of Israel, wandering in the

Nb 21:6

wilderness, were vexed by fiery serpents.* So those cloistered monks who should be the children of Israel indeed, but who wander at large in the wilderness of this world, are often in danger from envy. For that worm lives in ashes and dust; lying hidden in the dust, it stings to death. This is the rust which corrupts the treasure of wisdom, the locust which devours the fruits of the earth. For if any good work flourishes in a man, it consumes it. This is the vice which cast the angels out of heaven and shut man out of paradise. This infected the children of Israel in the desert. It

Gn 37:19
Gn 6

caused Joseph's brothers to take up arms against him.* It thrust Daniel into the lions' den.* In the end, it brought Our Lord to the suffering of the cross.

O man, what is your reward if you are envious? What does it profit you to be jealous? You prepare a snare; you dig it out. You yourself will fall into the hole you make. While you bind others to labor, you

are bound yourself. While you defraud others, you
deceive yourself. O man, you fight against nature;
you do battle with love; you trouble yourself; you go
astray from your duty to your neighbor and offend
God. You should rejoice in the joy of another, and
make another's grief your own by grieving with him,
and read your own wretchedness in the wretchedness
of another; you should understand the state of your
neighbor in your own person. Whither does envy lead?
Whither does jealousy take you? Whither does envy
bring you? It breaks the bonds of friendship, the ties of
charity, the contract of love, the law of natural justice.

CHAPTER IX: AGAINST ANGER

If the preacher wishes to arm a man against anger,
let him use these authorities: 'Everyone who is angry
with his brother, will be in danger of the Judgement'.*
Paul says: 'Do not let the sun go down upon your
anger'.* And James: 'An angry man does not do
justice'.† Solomon says: 'Fools show their anger at
once, but he who hides his anger is wise'* and: 'An
angry man provokes strife, but he who is patient
soothes ruffled feelings'* and: 'Anger lies sulking in
the heart of a fool'.* Gregory says: 'Who can bear a
spirit which is quick to anger?'[1] The psalmist says:
'Do not be angry, and sin not'.* The poet, too, tells
us: 'Anger is a brief storm; rule your spirit, for unless
it is obedient it becomes imperious. Hold it in check
with a bridle; curb it with chains'.* And Claudian:
'You bear the yoke of slavery if you are led by anger

Marginal references:
Mt 5:22

*Eph 4:26
[130]
†Jm 1:20
*Pr 12:16

Pr 15:1
Qo 7:10

Ps 4:5

Horace, Ep *1.ii.63*

---

1.   A misquotation of Pr 8:14, which is quoted by Gregory, *Moralia in Job* V:xlv; PL 75:724.

or fear, or if you desire what is evil'.[2]

See the authorities with which the Christian should
fortify himself against anger, as if with spiritual arms.
Behold how fertile anger is in bringing forth evil
progeny! From anger proceeds the rancor of hatred.
For what is hatred but old-established anger? From
that is born murder, insult, evil-speaking, injury.
O man, if you grow angry, if you hate your neighbor,
you contradict your very self when you cry to God in
prayer: 'Forgive us our sins, as we forgive those who
sin against us'. With what effrontery do you seek to
have your sins forgiven when you do not cast out from
your soul your hatred of your neighbor?

There are three kinds of anger. One arises in the
spirit, but does not come out into the open. This is
that anger of which it is said: 'He who is angry with
his brother will be in danger of the Judgement'.* For

Mt 5:22

even he who keeps his anger to himself will not escape
the judgement of eternal damnation. This anger is
signified by the daughter of the chief priest of the

Mk 5:22-43,
Lk 8:41-56

synagogue who lay dead on her bed.* There is another
kind of anger which goes as far as general quarrelsomeness; this is more serious, and closer to hell. On this
subject Scripture says: 'He who says to his brother

Mt 5:22

"Racha" will be in danger of the council',* that is,
he who is generally quarrelsome will be subject to a
more severe judgement. This is signified by the widow's

Lk 7:12

son.* For when one is provoked by anger to an actual
deed—something outside the mind—the 'dead' soul is
carried outside the 'gates' of the mind, to the actual
carrying-out of an evil deed. When indeed quarrelsomeness breaks out into particular villainies, this is an even
graver madness. Of this it is said: 'He who says to his

Mt 5:22

brother "Thou fool", will be in danger of hell-fire'.*

2.   *De IV. Con. Honor. Aug.* II:259-60.

The more serious the quarrels are, the more he who causes them is corrupted by the foul stench of infamy. If anger arises in the mind, it should be instantly bridled; little ones should be dashed against a rock before they grow; the little foxes should be captured before they damage the vineyard,* and the firstborn must be killed in the morning.* The Canaanite is cast out of the Promised Land.* Therefore, 'Do not let the sun go down upon your anger'.*

Jg 15:5
Ex 11:5
Ex 23:28
Eph 4:26

We must react to the first flickerings of anger in such a way that we not consent to sin. For it is human to be roused to anger, but it is diabolic to persevere in it. It is no shame to be roused to anger, yet not to sin. Hear what the teaching of your heavenly Master says: 'If you offer your gift at the altar and there remember that your brother has anything against you, leave your gift there', etc.* There you have it: if you wish to offer your material gift at the altar, you must first reconcile yourself with your brother if you have any rancor in your spirit, for the offering of an external gift profits nothing unless an inner peace of the mind is offered to God. Similarly, if you wish to offer on the altar of faith the sacrifice of a good work, first cast from your mind the clouds of rancor. If your brother has offended you, you must forgive him not seven times, but seventy times seven.* Our Lord Jesus Christ, in the moment of his passion, prayed for his tormentors,* and the first martyr, Stephen, interceded for those who stoned him.* If we are not so perfect that we are able to return good for evil, at least let us return no recompense for evil.

[131]

Mt 5:23-4

Mt 18:22

Lk 25:34
Ac 7:59

We should often bring to mind what the parables of the Gospel teach us. There we may read of him whose master forgave his debts, but who was not willing to let his own debtor go free. He was thrust into prison and forced to pay to the uttermost

Mt 18:34 farthing.* Similarly, the Great Creditor exacts the penalty for every single sin from the man who will not forgive his neighbor the injuries he has done him. When you let anger rankle in your spirit, you do not hurt your enemy, but you lose your own soul. You punish your own spirit through rancor, while you desire to vex someone else.

What malice is this? What vindictiveness, where, wishing to seize your enemy, you yourself are held fast; where, wishing to harm your enemy, you yourself perish? Attend carefully to this precept, and understand it well: 'Love your enemies and do good *Mt 5:42* to those who hate you'.*

CHAPTER X: AGAINST PRIDE

If he intends to inspire his listeners to flee from pride, let the preacher use these texts: 'Everyone who *Lk 14:11* exalts himself shall be brought low'.* And: 'What is valued highly among men is an abomination in the *Lk 16:15* sight of God'.* And Paul: 'Have no taste for self-*Rm 11:20* aggrandisement, but be meek'.* Jesus, son of Sirach: *Si 10:14* 'Pride is the beginning of every sin'.* Again: 'He has put down princes from their thrones, and he has *Lk 1:52* exalted those of lowly birth'.* Peter says: 'God resists *1 P 5:5, Jm 4:6* the proud but gives his grace to the humble'.*

O man, consider what pride may snatch from you, and what humility, the foster-child of the virtues, may *[132]* bestow. Pride made devils of angels, but humility makes man like the blessed angels. Pride was born in heaven, yet it lies low in dust and ashes. Let the cloister-dweller beware, lest he say with the Pharisee: *Lk 18:11* 'I am not like other men'.* Let him rather cry: 'I am a worm and not a man, an object of reproach among

Ps 22:7

Ps 12:5

Lk 18:13

Ho 14:6

Sg 2:1

Gregory, In Mt
25; *PL 76:1106*

Gregory, Super
Ps 38; *PL 79:
568-81*
*Lk 22:27

†*Si 3:18*

men and despised by the people'.* If he is an edu-
cated man, let him not chant with the Pharisee:
'Our lips are our own. Who is lord over us?'* But
rather let him cry with the Publican: 'Lord, be
merciful to me, a sinner'.* O man, it is for you to
take the lowest place; it is dangerous to stand on a
precipice. To the humble man the Lord says: 'I am
the dew, and Israel will blossom as the lily'.* The
lily grows better in the valley than on the mountain,
for there it is made more fertile by watering. It re-
tains its greenness longer and it preserves its whiteness
for a longer period of time. For this reason, it is
called 'the lily of the valley'.* So the true Israelite,
truly seeing God, is rooted in the valley of humility.
He grows the more freely because he receives a freer
watering of heavenly grace, and he blossoms the
better in spirit. He better preserves the splendor of
charity and the purity of innocence. For 'the more
anyone should be humbled by the gifts he has received, the more should he consider himself to owe a
debt in return'.* All works are without merit unless
they are seasoned with the sweetness of humility. For
he who acquires virtues without humility, throws—as
it were—dust into the wind.* This is the humility
which cries: 'Let him who is greater become like a
servant'.* And elsewhere: 'The greater you are, the
more you should behave humbly'.†

It is this which caused the Son of God to come
down from the bosom of his Father into the Virgin's
womb. This it is which wrapped him in cheap rags, so
that he might bestow on us the lovely garments of
virtue. It is this which circumcised him in the flesh,
that he might 'circumcise' us in the mind. This
allowed him to be flogged physically, that he might
free us from the flagellation of sin. This it is which
crowned our King with thorns, that he might crown

us with the roses of eternal blessedness.

O how different is pride from this humility! It cast Lucifer out of heaven, deprived Adam of Paradise, made Nebuchadnezzar into a beast.* This is the pride which insolently raises itself above its station, and descends below its appointed level into ruin. This is that which, while it seeks its own in what is beyond its reach, does not find itself within. It is pride which makes a man stand out among the common herd, and makes him an oddity in the community, a solitary in public, a man apart in the monastery. This it was that caused the fall of man, and it is the last thing which stands in the way of man's return to God. 'When you fight well, when you think all things are subjugated to you, what then stands in the way? Pride itself remains to be conquered.'* Pride makes a man's appearance affected, his actions immodest. As a result of pride, his words pour out in a flood, threats thunder forth. A man takes upon himself what is not his business, and neglects what is pressing. Pride handed the philosophers over to dishonest notions, blinded the Jews, destroyed the obstinate, cast down the exalted.

Pride is signified by the north wind when it is said: 'Arise, O north wind, and come, O south wind'.* The north wind is the enemy of flowers; it damages the corn; it freezes the waters into ice. So pride is a poor nurse to good and destroys the fruits of labor; pride freezes the mind in the ice of perversity. Of this it is said: 'From the north shall come every evil'.* For pride is the mother of all wickedness. It is also said: 'What do you see, Jeremiah? I see a seething pot boiling over from the north'.* This is the earthenware pot of the slaves of pride, in which the children of darkness are boiled—the hangers-on after honors, the seekers for riches, those who long for the highest seats,

Dn 4:13

[133]

See Textes, *261.*

Sg 4:16

Jr 1:14

Jr 1:13

l

and desire to be greeted respectfully in the market-
place and to be called 'Rabbi' by men. This pot
Nebuchadnezzar—that is Satan—kindled; to this he
set the fire of the feast of pride. In this pot the proud
man is boiled, and 'Egypt' eats the meal—that is, he
draws the unclean spirits into his body, and so he
bears them off to hell.

Pride is the wind which blows dust from the face
of the earth, for it casts out the proud man from the
security of everlasting life. This is that swelling which
a medicine cures, for pride does not accept the gift of
grace. There are four kinds of pride which blow
across the whole world like the four winds, for they
inflate the people of the world with swellings. They
are: arrogance, which imputes to itself what it lacks;
insolence, which takes to itself what it owes to others;
boasting, which credits itself with more than is true;
quarrelsomeness, which raises itself up against
authority. These are the four workmen who shake
the whole world and offer a variety of dreams
to men.

CHAPTER XI: ON DESPISING WORLDLY FEARS

Let the preacher who wishes to invite his listeners
to have contempt for worldly fear and to lead them to
seek a higher fear, make use of these authorities: 'Do
not be afraid of those who kill the body, but are not
able to kill the soul, but fear him who is able to
destroy both body and soul in hell'.* In the Book of
Wisdom we read: 'Fear God and keep his commandments'.* Elsewhere: 'Blessed is he who is always fearful'.* Again: 'The fear of the Lord is the beginning of

Mt 10:28

Qo 12:13
Pr 28:14

wisdom. At their end it will be well for those who
fear the Lord, and in the day of their death they will
be blessed'.* 'Those who fear the Lord keep his commandments, and are patient under his examination'.†
Jerome says: 'There is nothing which keeps us so safe
from sin as the fear of punishment and the love of
God'.* And Gregory tells us: 'To fear God is to leave
undone no good deed which ought to be done'.*

Si 1:13
[134]
†*Lk 1:52*

Source unknown
*Moralia in Job
1.iii; PL 75:530A*

From these authorities, he must proceed thus: O
man, you must particularly avoid every worldly fear.
It flees troubles before they come. It overemphasizes
the sorrow of its torments; in time of prosperity it
invents adversities, and it finds sadness and death
in joy. In times of uncertainty, it prophesies the
worst; it lies about the truth, and it abounds in falsehoods. No good thing is profitable to him who has it
unless his spirit is prepared to lose it.

Therefore, he who is Most Powerful encourages
you in the face of everything which can happen. Even
the ending of desire serves as a sound remedy for
fear, and, as Seneca says: 'Dread comes after hope. By
providence, the greatest good of the human condition
is turned to evil. Wild beasts flee the dangers they see,
when they can safely do so. We are tormented both by
what is to come and by what is past. Many of our
goods do us injury. For memory recalls the torment
of fear; it anticipates the working of providence. But
no-one is really so wretched in the present!'* O man,
overcome fear, which conquers all things! If you
overcome it, adversity will become prosperity, trouble
sweet, grief delightful.

Ep 5:7-9

O man, do you wish to put fear to flight and to
put away earthly things? Do not cling to earthly
things or care for what is transitory. If you love
earthly things, you are fearful of losing them or
of casting them away. If you wish to conquer fear,

fear God. Thus art is confounded by art, and thus a
nail is blunted by another nail.[1] Fear God so you will
not be afraid; serve God so you will not be a slave,
and observe his commandments in your mind. This is
every man—that is, for this was every man made—that
he might make out in himself every power of God.
Set yourself, O man, between two millstones, the
stone of fear and that of hope. Hope so much that
your spirit does not slacken, fear so much that your
thoughts do not wander. O man, do not fear the immi-
nence of death, nor hold back from the battle of life.
The one gives a just man greater merit; the other
increases his reward.

Do not think about how long you may live, but in
what manner. You must not take care that you live
long, but that you live a sufficiently good life. Living
long is a matter of chance, living well is a matter for

animus

the spirit.* Life is long if it is full. The spirit is 'full'
when it makes itself full of virtues, and does not
recoil from its own power. What profit is it to a man
if he spin out his life for eighty years by the sluggishness of an idle life? He has not lived, this fellow,
but merely lingered in life. Nor does he die at length,
but at last. But he who measures his old age by the
weight of his virtue, who extends with merit his
allotted span, he dies full of days; for even if he has
not reached his full number of years, his life is yet
complete.

[135]

I beg you, man, so to live that, as you know
what is precious to you hangs by a thread, so, too,
you may not doubt that the span of your life is hang-
ing in the balance. Let us measure by deeds, not by
time. A man recovers in a good deed what he lost in

---

1.   From the Greek proverb. See Aristotle *Politics* 1314a5 and Cicero
Tusculan Disputations 4:35:75.

passing. We do not suddenly cast ourselves into
death, but we proceed towards death bit by bit. We
die every day. Every day we shorten a little of our
life. Let us behave in such a way that the more our
temporal life diminishes, the more our eternal life
increases. What may be to the detriment of our
temporal life goes to increase our eternal life.

Let us arm ourselves with patience for life's course,
and for death's ambush. For we must be both coun-
selled and strengthened, that we neither love life too
much, nor fear too much the onslaught of death, but
weigh both in the balance of reason. For there is in
general an unthinking inclination of the mind
towards death. When certain men are weighed down
with sloth, they wish to end their boredom in death.
It is not the adversity of importunate worldliness
that should impel us towards death, but rather
the ardor of divine charity, that a man may not set
the end of his desire on the moment of death, but
rather on the bestowal of eternal blessedness.

CHAPTER XII: ON DESPISING THE THINGS OF THIS WORLD AND ON THE HOPE OF HEAVENLY THINGS

If the preacher wishes to invite his listeners to the
hope of heaven and to abandon the hope of earthly
goods, he should use these authorities, which
strengthen the one hope and draw the spirit away
from the other: for example: 'Cursed be the man
who puts his trust in man and relies on things of
flesh'.* Again: 'How hard it is for those who trust in
money to enter the Kingdom of Heaven'.* And

Jr 17:5
Mk 10:24

Ps 118:9
Ps 55:23
Ps 37:3

elsewhere: 'It is good to hope in the Lord rather than
to hope in princes'.* Again: 'Cast your thoughts on
the Lord, and he will sustain you'.* And: 'Hope in
the Lord and do good'.*

From these authorities he must proceed thus: the
hope of earthly goods leads only to promises for the
future; it destroys our joys before they arrive.
[Earthly hope] corrupts the mind by too much
anxiety, for fear trips up hope and mortgages the joys
to come; it stretches desire into infinity. O man, you
depend on earthly things; you rely upon what is
uncertain; you lean upon a reed cane which is easily
broken. Do not therefore trust in that which is fragile
and slippery; it quickly sinks away and destroys you.
Set your mind on the clouds of adversity rather than
on the clear skies of prosperity. If you set your hope
on earthly prosperity, that is deceitful and misleading.
When you grasp it, you will not find what you hoped
for. Learn from the prophet that hope is not to be
put in what is slippery. Why do you hope for that
which you cannot obtain at last—where you may not
find what you expect, where the pleasure is less when
it is experienced? Not only will you fail to find there
what you hope for, but you will discover instead the
tinder of sin and of ruin, a snare for your soul and the
leavening of justice.

[136]   Rather direct your hope towards tribulations, which
although they present an external bitterness, yet—for
those who stand firm—they bring forth in the spirit
the sweetness of the hope of heaven. Nor may he who
has not been pricked by the bitterness of tribulation
enjoy the sweet fruit of patience. Tribulation is the
furnace which refines gold, the file which burnishes
iron, the flail by which the grain is separated from the
chaff. In this warfare of tribulation, patience is exercised, fortitude does battle, constancy is strengthened,

hope is summoned heavenwards.

The anchor of hope should rather be dropped in
the harbor of salvation, in the mercy of the Saviour.
This hope does not confound, but restores. It illuminates; it does not blind. There, is found more than
is sought, more than hope can grasp. There, is more
than hope can understand. There, hope does not
devour joy, there fulfilment [of the promise] does
not diminish joy, for the fulfilment of the promise
leaves nothing to be awaited, where hope governs
your steps.

O how happy is that heavenly hope, which fear
does not overpower, in which fear is not engendered
by falsehood, where desire does not dream unde-
1 Co 13:7   tected, but, 'Love bears all, believes all, hopes all'.*
The utmost reaches of our reason invite us to believe
and hope in this. What fear is able to weaken the
human mind, if heavenly hope pleads for it before
God? What harm will the thunderings of tyrants, the
precipices of fortune, the weaknesses of the body,
the groanings of poverty do to the man whose mind is
fortified with heavenly hope? This is the hope which
governs the assemblies [of men], and directs their
actions. This it is which finds its height in charity,
that we may direct our actions towards God; this it is
which expands its breadth in charity, that we may
extend charity to our enemy. This it is which stretches
out its length in charity, that we may persevere in
charity to the very end of life.

Between this [hope] and fear, as between two
millstones, the Christian should be ground smooth
and fine. Whence it is said in Deuteronomy: 'You
shall not accept the upper or the lower millstone as a
Dt 24:6   pledge'.* The upper millstone is hope, the lower, fear.
The one must not be accepted without the other.
Anyone who hopes and does not fear is neglectful;

anyone who fears and does not hope is downcast.

CHAPTER XIII: OF SPIRITUAL SORROW

Anyone can lead men to spiritual grief by means
of these authorities and reasons: 'Blessed are those
who mourn, for they shall be comforted'.* And elsewhere: 'Woe to you who laugh now, for you shall
weep and mourn'.* James says: 'Be wretched, grieve
and weep. Let your laughter be turned to sorrow and
your joy to misery'.* Solomon says: 'It is better to
go to a house of sorrow than to a house of rejoicing'.*
Gregory tells us: 'Everlasting wailings follow present
joys. No-one can rejoice here with the world and
reign there with God'.*

There are three sorrows with which a man is bound
to flood his mind: sorrow for his own sins; sorrow for
others; sorrow for postponing heavenly bliss. The
first sorrow bears upon himself, the second on his
neighbor, the third on God. Of the first it is said: 'Tears
have been my bread, day and night'.* Of the second,
it is said: 'Who is sick, and I am not sick? Who is made
to stumble, and I do not burn?'* With this complaint,
Jesus wept over Jerusalem, saying: 'If you had known
—even you.'* Of the third complaint we read in the
Psalm: 'By the rivers of Babylon we sat and wept'.*
These are the lamentations of Jeremiah, with which
he bewails the sin of his soul, he bewails the indignity
of wretchedness and exile from his native land. With
the showers of such tears should a man water the
earth of his mind, that it may bear the fruit of good
works, and the various flowers of the virtues. These
are the morning dew and the evening dew; that is,
weeping for one's own sins, by whose watering there

Mt 5:5

Lk 6:25

Jm 4:9
Qo 7:3

Hom in Evang.
1,xi; PL 76:1117D

[137]

Ps 42:3

2 Co 11:29

Lk 19:42
Ps 137:1

springs up in the mind the seed of a good work. But
after the seed of repentance has come to the maturity
of perfect righteousness, the dew of evening should
fall, that is, weeping for the exile from one's native
land. Thus, by such a sprinkling with lamentation, we
may more properly measure the fruit of good works.
These are the waves of grace through which the children of Israel passed, going up into the Promised Land.
Sinners they left the Egypt of their vices, and first

Ex 14:28

they passed through the Red Sea,* in which their
enemies were drowned. That is to say, first they
passed under the waves of repentance, where the
errors of vice are washed away. For this reason we
should sing through our tears: 'Let us sing to the
Lord, for he is great and glorious; he has cast horse

Ex 15:21

and rider into the sea'.*

*Jos 11:17
†Num 21:15

After that, the children of Israel come to the
brook of Hermon,* and dangers lower.† When the
faithful are settled in the wilderness of the spirit and
snatched from the cares of the world and seated upon
the throne of the virtues, they weep for the sins of
others; they suffer with their neighbors; they consider
the errors of others to be their own, and so the dangers
lower over them. At last, the children of Israel come

Jos 3:17

to the Jordan, and cross over dry-footed,* as when
the faithful, brought to perfection, their spirits
cleansed from the waves of fleshly thoughts, are
overcome by tears at the dispelling of their present
wretchedness. The first is the weeping of repentance;
the second, of compassion for one's neighbor; the
third, of compassion for oneself. O man, see that
your mind is that book which Ezekiel saw, in which

Ezk 2:9

was written: 'Woe, lamentations and dirges'.* So, if
you were entangled in sin, may you be turned to
repentance, so, if the woe of mortal sin went before,
may tears of repentance follow—indeed, three

lamentations, a lamentation of repentance, a lamentation of compassion for others, a lamentation of grief for exile from one's native land. O man, turn yourself to utter these groans. Embrace these sorrows, and turn aside from other, earthly, sorrows.

If fortune is against you, do not let her hostility add to your sorrow. She has no means of hurting you unless you give her the power. Certainly, she cannot harm you, unless you injure yourself, and if you grieve you give her weapons. Why are you sad at the loss of those things which cause sorrow in the midst of pleasure? In the midst of peace, they cause dissension. Those things which ought to be a source of security, turn into a source of fear. If you ought to grieve for the death of a friend, you should grieve more for the danger to his soul, than for the loss of his earthly life. If you weep for him, you should shed the tears of your mind* for him before God, rather than a public wailing before the world. If natural weakness invites you to grieve, do not abandon your spirit* to grief. I do not forbid tears which necessity brings forth in the course of nature, tears which human weakness wrings out, for such tears slip out against our will. Often they flow for a friend at a time when wisdom prescribes them as a relief. Then tears lack neither humanity nor dignity. For it is right to give nature rein so long as propriety is preserved. But although nature invites you to grief of spirit,* do not let tears choke your spirit, but let your spirit stand steady and unmoved in the midst of tears. Let it hold firm in its wretchedness and let grief be mastered by the spirit. Let the mind contain its weakness, and let the spirit give little quarter to the flesh, or the reason to the senses.

If death threatens, do not grieve, but prepare yourself for its coming with steadiness of mind. So

[138]

mens

animus

animus

make yourself ready that you cannot fear death, and
that after death you may begin to live, you who,
before death, lived by dying. I do not say that you
should look to death as a refuge out of idleness, for
it is as vile at any time to fly to death as it is to flee
from death. Let the desire for eternal life invite you
to die; let the desire for greater merit detain you in
life.

Do not wish to be indebted to good luck, nor
choked by bad. Do not be one of those women whom

Ezk 8:14 Ezekiel saw weeping for Adonis.* Adonis we read had
died and after that was alive again, and over him when
dead the women seemed to grieve, and at his return to
life, they rejoiced. By Adonis is meant that earthly prosperity which vanishes at one moment and at the next
returns, because it is always changing and never stays
still. The women who grieved over his death and rejoiced
at his return to life, are those womanish men who are
forever being tossed about in the game of Fortune.
They grieve when Fortune grieves and smile when
she smiles. Those who have so many alterations of
mind, have as many changes of fortune. Such temporal grief is not to be embraced, but eternal sorrow
is heartily to be feared, where there will be weeping
without end, grief without respite, labor without
rest, there the whole soul will be in tears of conscience, and the whole body in a misery of wretchedness, for from the first gate on there will be wailing,
and from the second, wretchedness.

CHAPTER XIV: OF SPIRITUAL JOY

These authorities and reasons are able to lead a
man to spiritual joy: 'Rejoice in the Lord, O righteous

*Ps 32:11
[139]
*Lk 10:20
Is 25:9
Ph 4:4
Ps 66:1-2

men, and be glad'.* Again: 'Rejoice, for your names are written in heaven'.* And: 'We rejoice and are glad in you'.* 'Rejoice in the Lord always, and again I say, rejoice.'* 'Rejoice in the Lord all the earth; serve the Lord with gladness.'*

By these authoritative texts we are exhorted to spiritual cheerfulness of the mind. Great riches do not yield it, nor the deceptive glory of the world, nor earthly power, nor numerous offspring, nor bodily health, but a clear conscience and purity of life. No misery disturbs this joy, and no adversity destroys this prosperity; no bitterness mingles itself with this sweetness. O happy delight of a pure conscience, which drives out the worm within, frees the reason from the prison of sorrow and purges the mind of uncleanness!

This is the paradise of delights, planted with the many trees of good works, made colorful by the varied flowers of the virtues, watered by the spring of heavenly grace. This purity of conscience is the image of eternal life, and a prologue to the Kingdom of Heaven. Against this peace of mind, the Wheel of Fortune has no power.* Against this forearming of the mind the weapons of the world have no strength. He who has a clear conscience rejoices in the midst of grief, laughs in the midst of lamentations, is happy in adversity.

*Cf. Boethius,
De Consolatione
II, pr. 2.

This is the palace of Solomon, filled with diverse ointments, for in purity of heart the sweet gifts of grace give forth their fragrance. This is the resting-place of God, the royal abode of Christ, the couch of the heavenly Bridegroom. There the Bride, that is the soul, rests with Christ, her Bridegroom. There Rebecca runs to Isaac on his return from the fields.* There Jacob takes delight in the sweet embraces of Rachel.* There Mary Magdalen offers the most

Gn 24:65

Gn 29:30

jn 12:3
precious ointment to Christ.*

Cf. Virgil, Aeneid
1:604
O, if such is the happiness of a clear conscience,*
how great is the wretchedness of the branded mind!
By that judge no-one guilty is absolved; there the
worm of conscience remorselessly destroys the mind.
There the dire day [of Judgement] circles the spirit
Statius, Thebard
1:151
on remorseless wings,* there monsters throng, the
great freaks of sin. This is the book written by the
Devil's hand, defiled with hideous strokes; its page is
the mind conscious of evil. Its pen is the free will. Its
Cf. Misc. 11
ink is the enormity of sin.* There, O man, you call
wretchedly to mind whatever you have written from
your earliest youth, those matters in which you have
offended God, in which you have tripped-up your
neighbor, in which you have hurt yourself. O damnable book in which are written, not songs, but lamentations and dirges! But now, O man, erase by confession what you have written through false speech.
Erase by contrition what you have written through
evil thoughts. Erase by reparation what you have
written through evil deeds. Erase the book of a perverse conscience lest reason read there why it should
condemn you, lest the Devil find there grounds to
accuse you, lest God see there grounds to judge you.
[Erase it] that you may return to spiritual joy of
mind, that you may come to yourself, that you may
hasten back to God.

[140]

CHAPTER XV: ON PATIENCE

If you wish to teach your listeners patience, use
these authoritative texts: 'Patience completes its
Cf. Jm 5:7-8
task'.* 'Blessed are those who suffer persecution for
Mt 5:10
righteousness' sake.'* 'A man's teaching is to be

Pr 19:11 judged by his patience.'* And the philosopher says
that patience is highest virtue. It is through patience
that by dying the martyr rises above the living,
triumphs in suffering, finds delight in tribulation,
rest in labor. Patience brings syrup from gall, honey
from vinegar. The shield of patience shatters the
arrows of insult, and the virtue of tolerance repels
the darts of effrontery. There are four kinds of affront
which conquering patience defeats, and, by resisting,
it overcomes them. The first is the verbal affront,
which patience either absorbs into itself in the
tranquillity of silence, or softens by a gentle reply.
The second affront is that of hatred, which patience
remits, returning love for hatred. The third is the
affront of material things, which patience overcomes,
being content with small reward. The fourth is the
physical affront which is held at bay by the chastise-
ment of the flesh.

We read of many who had the aura of patience,
who claimed falsely to be steadfast, that they might
gain earthly prosperity. We wonder at certain animals
which pass through the midst of fire without injury
to their bodies. But we should wonder much more at
those who through cruelty pass unscathed and un-
harmed in spirit past sword and through catastrophe
and flames. It is base to give in to a passion, baser
still to surrender to it. To wrestle against it insures
that the battle need not be fought again if it is conquered. Enlarge your spirit; increase your strength;
no strong and energetic man avoids hard work. I say
that patience should have a place in the dealings
where a man engages himself in the cause of heaven's
business. In other matters, you will wear yourself out
by striving continually at what is unworthy. Why, if
you see weighty problems pressing in, do you not
turn your back and withdraw a step at a time to a posi-

tion of safety? It is easy to avoid the pricks of tribulation through patience, and it is easy, through
patience, to despise worldly goods. What is baser
than to be anxious under the roof of security itself?
This is the reason we become impatient, because we
are void of the heavenly good.

There are seven kinds of patience, which are
comprehended in the seven petitions of the Lord's
Prayer. The first counters the world's attack, the
desire for vainglory, the yearning for earthly doings,
the halter of greed. This we ask when we say: 'Deliver

Mt 6:13

us from evil'.* It is as though the faithful soul were to
say: 'Bestow on us patience against the evil of the
world, against the world's affronts.' Of this patience
it is saying, in the list of Beatitudes: 'Blessed are the
poor in spirit'.* For the first kind of patience con-

Mt 5:3

[141]

sists in the spiritual poverty which underlies the ab-
juring of external things, the putting from us of
nature's gifts, where a man, in putting from him those
things which belong to physical endowments—such as
strength, beauty, and so on—does not puff himself up
with pride in his natural endowments of soul.

The second patience is that which counters the
attacks of Satan. This kind of patience is what we
beg for when we say: 'Lead us not into temptation'.
A man does not ask not to be tempted, but that he not
be led into temptation—for someone may be tempted
without being led into temptation, as in the case of
the righteous man who resists the Devil. He who
gives way to malice is both tempted and led into
temptation, in that he sins. Of this kind of patience it

Mt 5:4

is said: 'Blessed are the meek'.* There comes the
highest meekness by this patience because a man does
not give his consent to the malicious Devil.

The third patience counters a neighbor's affronts,
when a man patiently bears wrongs done to himself.

Of this we speak when we ask: 'Forgive us our sins,

Mt 6:12 as we forgive those who sin against us'.* Of such it is

Mt 5:7 said, 'Blessed are the merciful',* for the spiritual workings of mercy lie in the forgiving of affronts.

The fourth kind of patience counters the trials of
natural poverty—that is, when someone sustains the
assault of want with a constant spirit. We speak of this

Mt 6:11 when we ask: 'Give us this day our daily bread'.*
What is this daily bread, but patience in the face of
poverty in the course of this life? For this
patience reckons a small sufficiency a great deal; it
feeds the mind abundantly, although it may not fill the
stomach. This patience makes fasting fruitful. In
coarse flour, it discovers the finest wheat, and it

Cf. Misc. 15 finds salmon in stockfish, spice in water.* Of this
it is said: 'Blessed are those who hunger and thirst after

Mt 5:6 righteousness'.* Patience which discovers satisfaction in physical fasting, hungers and thirsts for
righteousness. And the more it despises physical
food, the more it desires spiritual.

The fifth patience counters affronts to the flesh.
When someone manfully restrains the assaults of the
flesh, and chastises that beast of burden, that
sensuality may attend upon reason, and the flesh
the spirit, then the spirit holds dominion over the
flesh, and reason holds sway over against it. This
is the dominion we ask for in the Lord's Prayer,

Mt 6:10 when we say: 'Your kingdom come',* that is, 'Let all
things obey you'. So in us let sensuality obey reason.
Just as all things are peaceful in your kingdom, so in
the kingdom of our mind may all things be calm.
O how much to be feared is this duel between flesh
and spirit, when the flesh takes arms against the
spirit by the allurements of the senses, by the delights
of carnal pleasures! Behold the army of the flesh,
which prepares for war in its camp, and comes to do

battle with the spirit! It is the beauty of the thing which deceives the sight, the blandishment of sounds which seduce the ear, the sweet scents of things which confound the sense of smell, the flavor of food which attracts the sense of taste, the smoothness of the thing which excites the sense of touch. Against this army, patience arms the mind; it alone is able to fight off these enemies and to bring the quarrel to an end. It alone is able to restore banished reason to its kingdom. That war is more than a civil war, and thus the more to be dreaded. It is a foreign war, between man and the devil, of which it is said: 'For our wrestling is not against flesh and blood, but against the powers and princes of the air'.* There is a civil war between a man and his neighbor, of which it is said: 'The sons of my mother fight against me'.* It is a war more than civil between flesh and spirit, of which it is said: 'The flesh fights against the spirit, and the spirit against the flesh'.* This war can be settled by spiritual mourning, if one grieves for the loss of husband or wife, if one weeps at the onslaught of sin, if one mourns in the abstinence from carnal desire, if one weeps for the ending of earthly love. Of such grief it is said: 'Blessed are those who mourn, for they shall be comforted'.*

The sixth patience counters the miseries of the body which accompany labor: weariness, cold, heat, hunger, thirst. These are the wounds the robbers inflicted on the man going down from Jerusalem to Jericho.* That is, they are the demons of the sin of Adam, who went down from the Jerusalem of the heavenly vision, to Jericho, that is, into the fault of our mortality. Against this we have patience when the spirit finds virtue in sickness and in weariness, giving thanks to God, and so in the weakness of the flesh, discovers health of mind. When the mind finds

[142]

Eph 6:12

Sg 1:6

Ga 5:17

Mt 6:10

Lk 10:30

rest in labor, it offers up that punishment as its proper due, that those things which are weariness of the
body may be medicines of the mind. Against these
miseries of the flesh we ask patience when we say:
'Your will be done, on earth as in heaven'. That is:
'Grant that, just as in heaven (that is in the human
nature of Christ) your patience stood firm at the
behest of your will against these ills of the flesh, so,
too, on earth (that is, in us earthly men), patience
may be firm against the weaknesses of the flesh'. Of
this [patience] it is said: 'Blessed are those who

Mt 5:8   are pure in heart, for they shall see God'.* Through
this patience, the eye of reason is purged, lest through
weariness it fall into desperation, or through labor
slip into torpor.

The seventh patience counters the chastisements
of God by which He examines the righteous man,
proves his servant, and designates his son. For this
we ask when we say: 'Hallowed be thy name'.* For

Mt 6:9   when anyone is patient beneath God's chastisements
the name of 'son' is sanctified in him. And the more
patiently he bears God's chastisements, so much the
more is his Father's name sanctified in him, for the
Father chastises, through punishment, every son

Heb 12:6   whom he receives* through patience. Of this patience
it is said: 'Blessed be the peacemakers, for they will

Mt 5:9   be called children of God.'* For those who preserve
their peace of heart through patience while they are
chastised by the Father, are rightly proved the sons of
God.

[143]   If anyone therefore desires to be patient, let him
consider carefully the patience of Job, the death of
Christ, the constancy of the martyrs, and so let him
deride all the affronts of the world in the power of
patience. As we read in the book of Macrobius:
'Attacks upon the spirit are to be borne in the chains

of patience; great is his glory who is not swollen with

Source unknown   any praise, nor diminished by any insult'.* Plato says
of patience: 'We must so deal with pleasures that we
are safe against them—not by fleeing from them, nor
only when they are absent, but in such a way that we
defend our restraint and temperance with energy of
spirit and the habit of constant moderation. In the
same way, with a spirit warmed to the task, let us
melt away any frost of sadness, or langour of folly
which there may be in us.' Aristotle, too, says: 'Who,
possessing any human shame, congratulates himself
on sharing his pleasures with an ass?' Similarly,
Socrates[1] said that many men want to live so they
may eat and drink, and do not eat and drink so they
may live. Gregory, too, says: 'Do not impose on

Ps-Caecilius Balbus,   another what you yourself cannot bear'.* Socrates,
p.42. See Quadri,   again, says: 'It is the mark of wisdom to be careful
138.   not to fall into a snare, and if by chance someone
does fall in, to bear it bravely. For one cannot be
judged brave unless he is also wise; strength without

Balbus, p. 20   wisdom must be considered dangerous rashness'.*
And Socrates again: 'It is the mark of a good man to

Balbus, p. 39   know how to suffer, and to do no injury'.* Again:

Source unknown   'Patience is a refuge from wretchedness'.*

CHAPTER XVI: ON OBEDIENCE

By means of these authoritative texts, listeners
may be instructed in obedience: 'For us Christ made

Ph 2:8   himself obedient to death, even the death of the Cross'.*

1 S 15:22   Samuel, too, says: 'Obedience is better than sacrifice'.*

---

1.   Alan would probably have gathered these references to Plato and
Socrates from a florilegium source.

Again, the Apostle: 'Servants, obey your masters, and those who are set over you, not only those who are good and mild-mannered, but also those who are ill-tempered'.* 'He who resists authority resists a power ordained by God.'*

1 P 2:18
Rm 13:2

From these authorities one must proceed thus: O man, for our sake the Son of God was made obedient to the indignity of the Cross; are you not for your part willing to obey the precepts of the Gospel? When an angel obeys God in all things, do you, who are dust and ashes, defy God's law? Inanimate objects obey the Lord. You, who alone are endowed with reason, do you battle against God's will? The sun does not deviate from its course; the moon does not wander from its path; the stars shine in their appointed places. At God's bidding, the field grows lovely with flowers, the earth is watered with rain, the forest rustles with leaves, the little bird chirps in the glade— so all things obey the Lord. You alone battle against his laws. Consider, O man, that obedience is better than sacrifice, for through sacrifice another creature's flesh is destroyed; through obedience, your own will is offered up. The more quickly, then, a man makes his peace with God, the more his pride in his own will is suppressed; he sacrifices himself on the sword of the law. It is said that disobedience is like the sin of witchcraft,* and thus the greatness of the virtue of obedience is shown by contrast with its opposite. Of this obedience, Solomon says: 'The obedient man speaks of victory'.* For while we humbly submit ourselves to another's orders, we subdue ourselves in our own hearts.

lit. insensibilia

[144]

1 S 15:23

Pr 21:28

Yet we must know that obedience should sometimes not have its own way. When someone commands a position of greater importance, he casts away from himself the virtue of obedience in his eagerness to have

his way. But sometimes, obedience should retain
something of its own way, as when what is commanded is demeaning and shameful, for then a man
diminishes the goodness of obedience in himself by
stooping unwillingly to this summons, unless his
spirit desires these things of its own accord. Therefore
obedience should have some part in adversity, yet in
prosperity consider nothing its own. Thus Moses
Ex 3:11   humbly refused to be the leader of the people.* Paul
boldly says: 'I am ready not only to be bound in
Ac 21:13   Jerusalem, but also to die'.*

But you must beware lest you err in obeying.
You should therefore know that true 'obedience is a
virtuous decision of the spirit, the execution of a right
Source unknown   command with discretion'.* Mark the companions
obedience should have: that is, righteousness, that
what is commanded may be right. For this reason
it is said: 'The execution of a right command with
discretion'. Secondly, what is decided should be
honest: as it is said: 'a virtuous decision'. Thirdly, it
should proceed from discretion; for this reason is
added: 'with discretion'. That obedience which is
without discretion therefore is hollow. That which is
without honesty, is retrograde, for he who obeys
honestly, but out of an excess of obedience, shows
spiritual pride. If indeed obedience is without
righteousness, it is without law or principle.

We must know that evil should never come about
through obedience, but sometimes a good may be left
undone. Not evil was the tree in Paradise which God
forbade man to touch, so that through the merit of
obedience man might become blessed. Yet it was fit-
ting that he should forbid them this good. We must
take note of what is there said: 'From every tree of
Gn 2:16   paradise you may eat',* for he who forbids some
good to those set under him must allow many things,

so that the mind may not be turned away from everything and perish, as it were, from starvation.

There are four things which accompany reasonable obedience: discretion, honesty, righteousness, humility. There are, too, three kinds of rule of obedience: sufficient obedience, by which a man obeys his better; perfect obedience, by which a man obeys his equal; abundant obedience, by which he serves one lower than himself. The first is like the positive, the second the comparative, the third the superlative degree.* The first is by precept, the second a work of supererogation, the third a work of counsel. Christ fulfilled these three in himself, obeying one greater than himself when he obeyed the Father (whose inferior he was in respect of his humanity). He obeyed his equal, when he obeyed the Father in accordance with his divinity. He obeyed one lower than himself when he obeyed his mother.

[145]

A grammatical analogy of which Alan is fond.

Besides, there is a certain obedience which is straightforward, whose purpose is to act in accordance with a proper duty—as when, with good intention—we obey God. Another, which is right but not straightforward*, is when we obey God, but not in fulfilment of our duty. The Jew shows such an obedience to God his Creator, but his obedience lacks the character of duty, that is, the rule of charity and faith. A misdirected obedience is when we obey the Creator with an eye on human favor. [Obedience] is self-defeating when the devils obey God. For they obey in doing what they do not wish to do.

recta/directa

The first is meritorious, the second a mere beginning, the third self-seeking, the fourth, pernicious. The first is effective, the second active, the third deficient, the fourth destructive.

How effective is the rule of obedience which preserves harmony among the angels, which engenders peace among monks, without which the state cannot stand or the smallest household be ordered. The natural law of the beasts fulfils it, and the inanimate object keeps this law. By [obedience] the earth is bound to the skies, the divine to the human. This is the ladder by which the ascent to heaven is made. This above all: obedience nourishes humility, tests patience, scrutinizes gentleness.

Let the monk be eager to embrace obedience with the arms of charity. Let him render to God what is God's, and let him render to his neighbor what is his neighbor's. It is obedience which, according to the law of righteousness, renders to each what is due him.* And just as from obedience proceeds every good, so from disobedience arises every evil, as long as, through sin, man scorns obeying his Creator.

Cicero, De officiis 1.xviii.59

CHAPTER XVII: ON PERSEVERANCE

By these authorities a man is led to perseverance: 'He who endures to the end will be saved'.* Again, elsewhere: 'I say to you, even if he will not give to him because he is his friend, yet if he perseveres in knocking, because of his importunity he will arise and give him as many as he needs'.* The Apostle says: 'They all run the race, but only one receives the prize'.* And: 'He who has striven by the rules shall be crowned'.* In another place it says the same thing: 'That the Lord will judge the ends of the earth'.* And: 'Where a tree falls, whether to the south or to the north, there will it lie'.* Elsewhere we read that the outcome, not the battle, bestows the crown.*

Many tackle great tasks, but fail along the way. Many go out from Sodom, but quickly look back.*

Mt 10:22

Lk 11:8
2 T 2:5

2 T 2:5
Ps 10:8

Qo 11:3
Source unknown

Gn 19:26 [146]

Many leave Babylon, but die along the way and do
not arrive at the city of eternal peace, the heavenly
Jerusalem. Perseverance gives merit a shape; it colors
the intention of doing good; it rewards the runner
and crowns the warrior. It leads to the prize, it leads
to the harbor; it gives shape to the task and principle
to any action. This is Joseph's ankle-length tunic,
reaching to the end of life.* This is the priestly garment which reaches to the feet. This is the tail of the
sacrificial victim, which we are bound to offer to God.
This is the heel of a good work, which we should keep
safe from the serpent's bite.* This is the virtue which
informs every good vow, with whose laurels the martyrs are garlanded, and with which the virgins are
crowned. This it is which makes difficult tasks easy,
and overcomes every difficulty.* This is the garment
without crease, the spotless robe.† This it is which
makes a good action all one 'color', and virtue
uniform.

It must be noted that a certain kind of perseverance resembles grass which, like hay, in due time flourishes and withers in time of trouble. It blooms like a
flower, and is destroyed; it flees like a shadow and
never remains in the same state. Yet the ultimate
perseverance is that which endures to the end. This is
the cloistered garden, which has no contact with anything outside, the living fountain which always flows,
and gushes forth forever. The faithful strive to possess it, monks to preserve it, virgins to inform themselves by it, widows to persevere in it.

When the Devil incites a man to do good, he does
it so that he may entice him from good into a greater
evil. Perseverance is strong against this assault of the
Devil, and ensures that good beginnings may lead to
good ends: 'Lest the beginning be out of keeping with
the middle, or the middle with the end'.* To start out

Gn 37:3

Gn 3:15

*Reading facili-
tatem *for*
facultatem.
†*Cf. Eph 5:27*

Cf. Horace, Ars
Poetica, *152.*

well and to end in evil is to perform monstrous deeds.

That deed which begins in reason and ends in sensuality is like a chimaera; when this happens, 'The painter has joined a horse's neck to a human head'.* And so he introduces various plumes of fruitlessness. There are those whose life composes an amazing monster, whose beginning is good, as if it pretended to be the head of a man, whose middle part slips into dissipation and displays the belly of a goat, and whose end strays into grasping greed and has the feet of a wolf. O man, what profit is it to you to start out well and not to bring what you have begun to a proper end? 'It is better not to know the way of truth than, after knowing it, to turn back'.* Through this inconstancy, you will argue for what is fickle, run into apostasy, put from you constancy of mind. Seneca says: 'It is the nature of an orderly mind to be able to rest in the good and dwell there. Nothing is so useful that it can be profitable to change it'.*

A corruption of Horace, Ars Poetica, *1-2.* Cf. *Ad fratres in eremo, Sermo 8; PL 40:1249-50.*

2 P 2:21

Cf. Ep 2:1 and 3.

[147]

Perseverance trains a good man, and leads the tender child to maturity. It looks not for a childish, but for an adult, spirit. It looks for mature behavior, not for what is immature or outrageous. If perseverance does not adorn the whole of life, let final perseverance at least bring it to its conclusion. If you have handed over the flower of your youth to the devil, at least offer the dregs of old age to Christ. In the evening, the tranquillity of the day is praised; and at its end, the steadiness of good work.

See from how great a good Judas fell. He did not persevere in good. See what Solomon lost through inconstancy of Spirit, and into what calamity Saul fell. We can guess how great is the merit of perseverance from the infamy of its opposite vice—that is, failure to repent. It is said of failure to repent, that such is the stain of this sin that it cannot be pardoned

at a humble petition. For this is the sin against the
Holy Spirit, this is the mortal sin of which John says:
'There is a sin unto death; I do not say that one

1 Jn 5:16 should pray about that'.* Yet failure to repent is born
of desperation, or it arises out of presumption, and—
as much as in it lies—it either detracts from the
righteousness of God or diminishes his mercy. Happy
then is perseverance, which removes the failure to
repent, casts out stubbornness, throws away contempt, and wipes out hardness of heart.

CHAPTER XVIII: ON MERCY

These authorities can summon a man to mercy:
Mt 5:7 'Blessed are the merciful, for they shall obtain mercy'.*
Mt 9:13 'I desire mercy and not sacrifice.'* On the same sub-
ject: 'Blessed is the man who is merciful, and accommo-
Cf. Mt 5:7 dates himself to others'.* And James in the canonical
Jm 2:13 Epistle: 'Mercy triumphs over judgement'.* Solomon
the same: 'Mercy and truth protect the King, and his
Pr 20:28 throne is made more secure by clemency'.* And in the
Gospel: 'Everything which you wish men to do to you,
Mt 7:12 you do to them; this is the law and the prophets'.*
O man, if you consider carefully the mercy of God,
you can possess in yourself the image of mercy. What
made Christ become incarnate, except mercy? What
subjected him to our wretchedness, except his clemency? This is man's only way to God, and God's to
man. O blessed way, which alone knows the exchange
of our salvation, which alone points man up to God,
and brings God down to man.
This alone is the mediator which reconciles
adversaries, brings together those who are separated,
makes the unequal somehow equal, humbling God,

raising us, drawing him into the depths, and lifting us
into the heights. Yet this happens in such a way that
his coming down is not demeaning to him, nor is our
exaltation proud but glorious. For mercy has great
force; it alone was able to bring God down from
heaven to earth, and lead man back from exile to his
native land. O great chain of mercy, by which God
could be bound and man, bound by the chain of
iniquity, set free!

[148]

O man, if you contemplate your wretchedness,
you will find nothing but mercy in the works of God
towards you. It is a mercy if he restrains the sinner, if
he chastises him that he may mend his ways, if he
frees him from sin, if he keeps him in justice; it is
mercy, too, if he punishes him eternally, for that is
less than what has been deserved; it is mercy if he
gives an everlasting reward, for he rewards beyond
what has been deserved.

Nor is his justice thereby diminished, for his justice
demands the exercise of mercy. Justice should always
have mercy as its companions, for the truth of justice
turns into severity unless it is seasoned with the
sweetness of mercy. Whence it is said: 'Mercy and
truth have met together, and justice and peace have

Ps 85:11

kissed one another'.* Justice should, as it were, kiss
mercy, that it may not wander from the path of
mercy, nor mercy stray beyond the bounds of
justice.

For this reason, judgement is said to lie upon the
altar of mercy, for justice is crammed into an abyss of
cruelty if it is not tempered by the grace of mercy.
Mercy is the seasoning of justice, the medicine of
judgement. Toward wretchedness, however, mercy
ought not to be either commonplace or abrupt; as
Seneca says: 'It is as much a cruelty to pardon all

Source unknown

as to pardon none'.* Much damage is done by

severity and by mercy, if one is employed without the other, but this should be the practice of rulers concerning those who are set under them: both justly to console with mercy, and righteously to correct with severity.

Let us reflect on how much Moses loved his people, for whose life he asked that he might give his own; with what a zeal for righteousness, what he had obtained forgiveness, did he say to the people: 'Let each man gird his sword upon his thigh'.* Behold, he who begged for men's life with his own death, snuffed out the life of few men with his sword. Within, he was inflamed with the fire of love, and without, with zeal for severity before God. Brave ambassador of both, he pleaded the cause of the people before God with prayer and the cause of God before the people with the sword.

O man, may you pursue mercy towards your neighbor eagerly, at the prompting not of fortune, but of the cause itself. Let not weakness of spirit, but the love of God, awaken clemency. For there are many who are moved by the tears of the most wicked men who—if they were allowed—would break out of prison. Not love, but feebleness of spirit, moves them. Therefore let charity bestow compassion on men, and let equity punish the enormity of vice.

It is especially important, in the works of mercy, to make sure that the hungry man is fed, the thirsty refreshed, the naked clothed, the wanderer given shelter, the orphan comforted, the sick visited. These are the works of mercy, which the righteous man distributes in judgement, and which will be pleaded on his behalf on the Day of Judgement. The works of mercy alone will plead for a man in his last cause. For 'Judgement is without mercy towards those who have shown no mercy'.* O man, recognize yourself in the

Ex 32:27

*Jm 2:13, cf.
Mt 26:35-41*

wretchedness of another; in other things, behold your
own wretchedness. If you are righteous, you can fall.
If you are rich, it is the gift of fortune, not of nature.
If you are healthy, sickness is either imminent, or it

[149]   threatens you closely. If you are wise, the wisdom of
man is not reliable.

O man, if you wander from the path of clemency,
you muddy the fountain of mercy—as much as it lies
in you to do so. You who have some experience of
the fountain of mercy and of piety in God, at least
allow a trickle of mercy to run out upon your neighbor. What will happen if your Saviour is merciful and
holy, and you are harsh and merciless to your neighbor? You have received mercy from the Lord, and do
you inflict malice on your neighbor? You can read in
the mercy of God what you should do, what principle
of clemency you may best apply. And certainly, you
are bound to embrace mercy rather than justice.
Every man should tend naturally to mercy rather
than to justice, for mercy gives rise to love and justice

1 Jn 4:18   to fear. Because love drives out fear,* love is worthier
than fear. There are many things which advise us to
temper justice a little: the weakness of human nature,
the profitableness of the matter, and the dignity of

Jm 2:13   mercy, which is more jubilant than justice.* Let
mercy then be born, not from negligence, nor from
feebleness, nor from indiscretion, nor from weakness
of spirit, but let it be circumspect in every way, that
it may preserve what is its own, and not misappro-
priate what is due to justice.

Behold, O man, in Joseph, a mercy which forgot

Gn 43   his brothers' injury.* Read of the grace of clemency
in David who wore himself out bemoaning the madness

2 S 18:33   of his scheming son.* Set these examples before you,
and others like them, if you wish to follow rightly the
path of mercy. If you shut up your feelings of mercy

from him who is in need, you shut upon yourself the door to the mercy of Christ. For mercy is the key with which Heaven is opened, and it absolves the guilty. This is the gateway of the Lord; the righteous shall enter in through it. This is the mercy which illumines the New Testament, and moderates the rigor of the Old Law. This is the wood which made the waters of Mara sweet;* with this salt Elijah purified brackish waters.* With this meal, Elijah took away death from the earthenware pot.* This oil did the Samaritan pour upon the wounds of the wounded man.*

Ex 15:25
2 K 2:20-2
2 K 4:40-1

Lk 10:34

Clemency makes a man not only honorable, but safe. Clemency is the adornment of princes and the steadiest light. This alone distinguishes between the cruel and the pious, between king and tyrant. The king is armed with clemency. The tyrant by his arms provokes hatred. O man, how would you make satisfaction, unless clemency came to your aid? If God were to treat you with strict justice, the punishment which he would match to your deserts could not be imagined, nor could the pleadings which would balance your offences. Therefore ascribe all things to God's mercy, and lavish mercy on your neighbor in like manner. Do not be a miser in compassion, for you have known the generosity of mercy in God.

CHAPTER XIX: ON JUSTICE

These authorities exhort men to justice: 'Love justice, you who judge the earth'.* On the same subject: 'I have dealt judgement and justice; do not give me up to those who slander me'.* Again: 'Blessed is the

Ws 1:1
[150]
Ps 119:121

man who dwells on wisdom, and who meditates on

Si 14:22 justice'.* Again: 'Judge in favor of the fatherless and
the oppressed, that man upon earth may lord it over
Ps 10:18 them no further'.*

O man, you must take care over the principles
upon which you do justice, lest you sharpen judgement out of hatred, or intensify it out of cruelty, or
moderate it out of love of money, or abridge it out of
fear. Let the fine clothes of the rich man influence
you no more than the rags of the poor. Take the
Cf. Num 21:22 royal road,* and turn neither to the right—by
softening your judgement—nor to the left—by sharp-
ening the punishment. It is not cruelty to punish the
guilty, but justice; it is not the act of a tyrant, but the
judgement of divine righteousness.

But beware, lest you cast out the speck from an-
Mt 7:3, Lk 6:41 other's eye and fail to see the beam in your own.* Do
not desire to reveal someone else's small failing so that
you may ignore your greater fault. Do not be so
anxious about another's slight indisposition that you
put out of your mind your more serious illness. To
Lk 4:23 you it may be said: 'Physician, heal thyself'.* Hear
what the Lord says to the Pharisees who accused the
woman taken in adultery: 'He who is without sin, let
Jn 8:7 him first cast a stone at her'.* If you, a sinner, condemn another sinner, you condemn yourself. O man,
with what effrontery do you accuse another of that
which you find more gravely wrong in yourself? With
what barefacedness do you judge your neighbor,
when you know you should be judged more severely?

Becoming to a prince is a justice circumcised from
every vice, circumscribed by deserved bounds, surrounded by its fellows. That righteousness may go
hand in hand with justice, let it not deviate in judgement from the right. Let it be accompanied by discretion, that it does not make mistakes. Let it go hand in

hand with charity, that it may wield the sword of
retribution with the zeal of justice, not with the
rancor of hatred. It should be exercised with mercy, lest
'justice' turn out to be cruelty; with deliberation, the
judge considering and thinking over his sentence at
length. So it is that Seneca says: 'It is not surprising that
you condemn freely, if quickly, and punish those beneath you harshly, because excessively. It is a praise-
worthy thing to rule with moderation.' Nature makes
it clear who is king, by distinguishing him from the
other animals over whom nature has set him as king—
as among bees. Nature does not wish him to be violent,
nor to seek by his greatness a remorseless revenge.
She withdraws his power from him, too, and leaves
him defenceless, for, as Seneca says, bees are extremely
savage and fierce in attacking the body, and they
leave their stings in the wound. The king himself has
no sting, and in this respect he affords an example
for the great.

    Let it shame a prince not to model his own
behavior on that of these creatures. For the greater
its power to injure, the more restrained should a

Cf. Seneca, De
clementia *1:14:3
& 18:1, cf. 19:2-4*

man's spirit be.* He who is endowed with justice will
cross the Red Sea—the sea of earthly vices—dry-footed

Ex 17:6

with Moses. This is the rod which caused a spring to
flow when it struck the rock,* and which causes
rivers of virtue to leap forth from the stony hearts of
those subject to it. This is the winnowing-fork by
which grain is separated from the chaff; the furnace
in which silver is isolated from dross metal; the sword
by which the living is divided from the dead; the
instrument by which the healthy person is separated
from the diseased, for to cure the disease of sin, a
stinging poultice must be applied, lest the unhealed

[151]

corruption of the vices should burst forth, and, in the
increase of evil deeds, unpunished iniquity should

be reinvigorated.

This is the measure with which we should mete out punishment and weigh a man's deserts. This it is which accords justice to everyone and serves the common good. For sometimes part of the penalty must be remitted to avoid causing a stumbling-block to others; sometimes the punishment must be increased, to give warning to others. This is medicine for the vices, the antidote to sin. This is the sword which defends both parts of a man—the body against external injuries, the soul against inner vexations. This is the stone with

1 S 17:49 which David struck down Goliath* and freed Israel from slavery. Without discretion this is a sword in the hand of a madman; without power this is a sword in the hand of a cripple; without mercy, this is a sword in the hand of a tyrant. The exercise of justice requires the highest discretion, that we should not judge on grounds of suspicion, but rather base it on righteousness. Condemn no-one without a hearing. Try the case first, and then give judgement. For it is not he who is accused, but he who is found guilty who is to be condemned.

CHAPTER XX: ON THE LOVE OF GOD[1]

These authorities set forth the nature of love: 'Love the Lord God with all your heart and with all your

Mt 22:37 soul'.* John says: 'God is love, and he who dwells in

---

1. On Alan's 'vocabulary of love' cf. R. T. Otten, '*Amor, caritas* and *dilectio:* some observations on the vocabulary of love in the exegetical works of St. Ambrose' *Mélanges offerts à C. Mohrmann* 73-83, and H. de Sainte-Marie, 'Le vocabulaire de la charité dans la règle de S. Bénoit', *ibid.,* 112-20.

1 Jn 4:16   love lives in God, and God in him'.* Peter, as well: 'Above all, have mutual love for one another, for love

1 P 4:8   outweighs a multitude of sins'.* And Paul: 'Love is

1 Co 13:4   patient and kind'.* Augustine, too: 'Everything we do without love benefits us nothing, and in vain do we dissipate our energy if we do not have love,

Source unknown.   that is, God'. Gregory† says: 'The more the heart of
†the Great   the sinner is consumed with the fire of love, the more

Hom. in Ev. *II, 33;*   it is purged of the rust of sins'.* From these texts, we
PL 76:1241 C   must continue thus: Who, even armed with the eloquence of Cicero[2] and filled with all wisdom, can adequately sing the praise of love and expound its virtues? It is love which teaches us to flee enticements, to tread pleasures under foot, to subdue the lusts of the flesh, to despise marks of deference, to crush illicit desires and, finally, to renounce all the blandishments of this life. On this subject, the Bridegroom declares in the *Song of Songs:* 'Set me as a seal upon your heart; set me as a seal upon your arm, for love is

Sg 8:6   as strong as death, and jealousy as cruel as hell'.* For death snuffs out the living, and hell does not spare the dead. Love, then, is like death, for just as the one subdues the senses of the flesh, so the other subdues

affectum   the movements* of carnal desire. Envy is cruel as hell, for it obliges those whom a longing for eternity draws inward not only to spit out smooth things,

[152]   but also to put up with harsh and bitter things in attaining what they love. Love braces the other virtues with the fortifications of its perfection. Whoever roots himself in love will fail neither to flourish nor to bear fruit, for he lives so as to be productive. On this matter Isidore* says: 'No reward is of value without the love of charity, and no matter how

---

2.   This reference to the eloquence of a Cicero is a conventional compliment, offered, for example, to both Lanfranc and Anselm.

strongly one believes aright, he cannot come to
blessedness without charity'.* For such is the power
of love that even prophecy and martyrdom are of no
avail without it. Of all the virtues, love holds first
place. For this reason, the Apostle calls it the chain of
perfection,* for all the virtues are linked together by
the chain of love.

Cf. Isidore of
Seville
Sententiae *II.3.2;*
PL 83:602.

Col 3:14

Love God, then, that you may be loved by him,
and conduct your life so that you may the more
swiftly come to him, for through love you will grasp,
possess, and enjoy him. This is the most excellent
way, the highway, which straightens winding ways,*
and clearly indicates the direct ways. This is love
which so moved God that it led him from the seat of
highest majesty to the lowliness of our mortal nature.
It wounded him who could not suffer, it moved him
who could not be changed, it bound him who could
not be conquered, it made mortal him who is
eternal.

Cf. Mk 1:3

If love was able to do so much in God, how much,
O man, should it be able to do in you? If God bore so
much for man, what shall man refuse to bear for God?
Let it shame a man not to be subject to love, which
subjected the Creator of the world to itself. Love
does not envy, it does no wrong, but it tears out the
root of vice from him in whom it dwells. Love is the
source of all virtue; it illuminates the mind, purifies
the conscience, rejoices the soul, shows forth God.
Pride does not puff up the soul in which love dwells,
nor does envy rack it; anger does not destroy it; evil
and sadness do not trouble it; lust does not pollute it.
gluttony does not inflame it; lust does not pollute it.

Love is always chaste, always pure, always quiet,
always kind; strong in adversity, steady in times of
prosperity. This is the spiritual cross, and anyone who
lays hand on it to take it up and carry it, follows in

the footsteps of Christ. Its height reaches up to God, its breadth is stretched out towards the enemy, its length to the end of life, its depth savors the immen- sity of divine grace.* This is charity, which is the shield of the warrior, the reward of the victor, which so sets out on the road that it may come to its end in its homeland. It is a fire in Sion, and a forge in Jeru- salem.* Love brings forth as it were a created Trinity in which the love of God is like the Father, from whom proceeds the love with which man himself is loved, as a child by his Father. From both proceeds the love of one's neighbor, just as the Holy Spirit proceeds from both [Father and Son]. Again, three distinctions lie in the single substance of charity, and they are different in their individual properties.

Beware, O man, if you would pursue love, lest you are fooled by a shadow of love. For there is the love of fortune, which comes with prosperity. With this, carnal man loves God when things go well for him. There is the love of nature by which every reason- able creature loves God. As the blessed Augustine says: 'No one's mind could ever hate God'.* There is the love of grace, which alone has merit; by it God is loved so that he may be enjoyed as its reward. The first wears out, the second wears well, the third wears perfectly. The first is of the flesh, the second of the senses, the third of the reason. The first is the love of a false brother, the second of the humble sinner, the third that of the man who is justified. O man, consi- der how sweet is the love of God, how impure is the love of this world. The love of God is the mother of all virtues; the love of the world is the mother of all vices. With that love, all things are imperfect. With this, all things are brought to perfection.

Through love, God is desired with the whole heart, sought before all things, found beyond all things,

Cf. Misc. *1 & 3*

Is 31:9

[153]

Source unknown

loved above all things. This is the fire which God
Lk 12:49   came to bring upon the earth,* that it might burn
away the rust of sin, and burn up the chaff of vices.
In the heights love has set up his camp, which worldly
fear, earthly love, the hopes of the flesh, the sadness
of adversity, cannot defeat. For who can perceive its
breadth, which is extended even to its enemies? Who
can comprehend its height, which stretches up to
God himself? Who can behold its depth, which reaches
to the depths of divine wisdom? 'God is Love, and
1 Jn 4:16   he who dwells in love lives in God and God in him'.*
Hear, O man, and lest you value too little the possession of love, hear that Love is God; surely it is no
small thing to have God dwelling in oneself? Surely it
is a great thing to have love in yourself, for Love is
God. This privilege Love alone has—that it may be
called, and indeed be, God; it can fit no-one else, for
though all virtue is God's gift, none but love alone has
this: thus it is not only God's gift, but may also be
called God himself.

CHAPTER XXI: ON THE LOVE OF ONE'S NEIGHBOR

Mt 22:39,   A man may be taught to love his neighbor by these
Mk 12:31   authorities: 'Love your neighbor as yourself'.* 'What-
Mt 7:12   ever you wish men to do to you, you do to them.'*
Lk 6:35   'Love your enemies; do good to those who hate you.'*
Sixtus, too, says: 'The foundation and the starting-
point of the worship of God is to love our fellow
Enchr. 371   men'.* St Gregory: 'It is true love if one loves a friend
in God, and for God's sake loves an enemy. God him-
self is not loved if you have no love for your neighbor,
nor is the neighbor himself loved, without love for

Hom. in Ev. *I.ix;*
PL 76:1108.

Source unknown
[154]

God'.* Again, Bede: 'Love is said to be that which
binds two, God and man, or unites one neighbor
with another'.* For although the love of God is
greater in love's merit, yet the love of neighbor is
greater in its effect, because through the love of
neighbor one comes to the love of God. O man, love
your neighbor as yourself; the good things which you
desire for yourself, you should not begrudge to others.
If you hope for more for yourself than for another,
you are envious; if more for another than for yourself, you are foolish. Ponder nature; she will teach
you to love your neighbor as yourself. For she has
made all things common, and she has made one origin
for all, for: 'Every race of men is descended from a
like origin'.* If you deny to another what you wish
to be done for yourself, you war against nature, and
refuse a common right.

Boethius, De
consol. phil. *III,*
metr. vi. 1.

You should lay on no one burdens which you
yourself cannot bear; show to others what you would
wish to be shown to you. How can you despise your
nature in another, when you embrace the same thing
in yourself? Every animal loves his own kind, and so
should every man love his neighbor. All flesh is con-
joined with the company of its own kind. The Samaritan of the Gospel, although he was a stranger to the
wounded man, yet he cared for the sick man; and
how can you not love your neighbor? Be therefore a
friend to every neighbor in time of persecution, and
not only in time of prosperity. Be a friend not of the
table, or of good fortune, but of tribulation, that
you may make another's troubles your own by suffering with him, and that you may make his grief
your own by grieving with him. What greater love is
there than to lay down your life for your friends and
to extend love to your enemies?

These are wonders in the law of God. Just as God

takes pity on his creature; so do you show mercy to your nature in your neighbor. How much is love to be praised when it binds neighbors together, joins those who differ, brings unity to plurality, restores identity to diversity? This is the concord of disharmonies, the unity of plurality, consenting dissent, diversity joined. This is the robe of Christ woven seamless from the top throughout.* This is Joseph's coat of many colors.* This is the diversity of patterns in which we read that the queen was robed, of whom it is said: 'At your right hand stands the queen in golden robes, embroidered round about with many patterns'.* Of this unity of charity it is said: 'Behold how good and joyous it is for brothers to dwell at one'.* 'At one' means not 'in one place', but 'of one mind'. For to dwell in a single place and not to be of one mind is a punishment, not a delight. This oneness leads on to heavenly unity, of which it is said: 'One thing have I asked of the Lord, this I require'.* This unity makes a man rich in his neighbor's wealth, makes him glad in another's joy, and leads especially to this common good, that he should increase another's good, not destroy it. Let it shame Christians not to be linked to one another by the chain of love, when we read that even the pagans were bound as equals to one another in friendship, by the very bond of natural love. If earthly love makes many one in friendship, shall heavenly love* not bind the faithful in the bonds of charity? If in many cases frivolous reasons give birth to friendship, may eternal rewards not do the same? O what sweetness lies in the true love of one's neighbor, which neither human favor, nor earthly convenience, nor human flesh, but love alone brings forth! This it is in Samuel which prayed for Saul.* This it is in Moses which pleaded for the people to God.* This weeps in David for Jonathan,† and in

Marginal notes:

Jn 19:23

Gn 37:3

Ps 45:10

Ps 132:1

Ps 27:4

[155]

reading amor
for amore

1 S 15

Ex 32:11
†*2 S 1:12*

Lm passim   Jeremiah for Jerusalem.* Certainly he who cuts himself off from the love of his neighbor strays from the
love of God, for: 'Anyone who does not love his
neighbor whom he has seen, how can he love God
1 Jn 4:20   whom he has not seen?'* O man, surely, you wish
that your neighbor should love you for God's sake?
Love him for your own sake. As Seneca, the moral
Ep 9:6   philosopher, says: 'If you wish to be loved, love'.*
O happy love, which external causes do not move,
and which is truly grafted into the nature of the
highest good, which is content without envy. Such
love possesses its delight within itself; it does not
grow anxious; it rests in tranquillity. It does not
dissolve into mockery. O how joyous it is to find
your very self in another! It is indolence and negligence to let the employment of love fall into disuse,
and not to exercise the most noble of the virtues.

It is the glory of true friendship to be the instrument of purging the last dregs of merely superficial
delight. You have a friend, not so that he should visit
you when you are sick, or feed you when you are
famished, or comfort you in prison, but so that you
should visit him in prison, feed him when he is hungry, give him drink when he is thirsty; if he is a
wanderer, take him in. If you love a poor neighbor,
you give him alms out of love alone, for the alms of
the heart are much greater than that of the body. Love
alone is enough, in almsgiving, without earthly substance. That which is given physically is not enough,
unless it is bestowed in a kindly spirit. Keep therefore
to the order of love. Love God above all, yourself
next, and your neighbor as yourself, the flesh least
of all.

Love the flesh, not so that you may be its slave,
but so that you may set it right with discipline. Love
it for its good, not for the sake of worldly debauchery.

Do not heed its will, but force it to heed yours. Like
a good doctor, cure by this means what is weak,
broken* or diseased. So let it grieve now that it may
rejoice in eternity. Let it now taste the bitterness of
medicine, that the soundness of eternal health may
follow.

fractum;
PL=factum

CHAPTER XXII: ON PEACE

The following authorities teach peace: 'Peace I
leave with you; my peace I give to you'.* On the same
subject: 'Be at peace among yourselves'.* Again:
'Blessed are the peacemakers, for they will be called
the children of God'.* Of peace is also said: 'Peace,
which passes all understanding'.* And: 'Glory to God
in the highest and peace on earth towards men of
goodwill'.* Gregory says: 'If we show how great
is the virtue of peace, which we must cherish eagerly,
we know . . . ' etc.* We know the worth of this virtue
well enough, however, because our Lord and Redeem-
er deigned to bequeath it to his disciples as a great
gift, that by it those who share with him in his peace-
making might with him be peacemakers. And so states
the law of nature; the elements, the planets and other
inanimate things are embraced in his peace.*

Jn 14:27
Mk 9:49

Mt 5:9
[156] Ph 4:7

Lk 2:14

Source unknown

illius pacis;
PL=ulnis pacifice.

There are three kinds of peace: the peace of our
time, peace of heart, and the peace of eternity. The
first is the shadow of peace, the second the concomi-
tant of peace, the third the substance of peace. In the
first are the dregs of peace, in the second its leavings,
in the third a feast of delights. The first is an ima-
ginary peace; the second is a summons to peace, the
third a substantive peace. The first peace consists in
worldly prosperity; the second proceeds from

tranquillity of mind, and the third emerges in the joy of heavenly life.

The first peace is not to be desired, because it is deceptive, elusive, and transitory, and when it is thought to be possessed, it flees away. This is a womanish raging, prosperous adversity, bitter sweetness and sweet bitterness. This peace sends clouds upon serenity, tumult into tranquillity. In the likeness of worldly good it bewitches; then it grows wild like the sea—now it is tranquil, then suddenly it is stormy and, as Seneca says, on the same day that the ship sets sail, it goes down.* The pleasures of this peace both princes and paupers experience, as do those between. Anyone who hopes for it plants his foot in a slippery place, steers his boat into shipwreck, stands on a precipice, sows on arid ground.

Ep 4:7

The second peace is far more excellent than the first. It does not fear the slickness of a merely outward peace; it does not tremble at the clouds of fortune; it cleanses the mind of vices. The worm of conscience does not destroy it; the threats of princes cannot dispel it, nor do the attacks of the enemy drive it away. With this companion alone, a man is rich; with this alone a wise man is content, with this companion he is safe in adversity, secure in dangers. This peace makes a man the son of God. It encourages him to store up virtues and to drive out vice. Of this it is said: 'In peace will I both sleep and take my rest'.* In this peace of mind is a tranquil sleep, peace and quiet, true vision. He whose mind depends on outward goods does not possess this peace. He who is not content with himself, lacks such peace. He who is at peace within himself is at peace with his neighbor. No-one can enclose it within if he does not put it into practice outwardly.

Ps 4:9

This peace of eternity is that which surpasses

[157]

Ac 8:9,13
Ex 20:10

all peace, where God is all in all, all things are One,
and One is all in will. There the flesh does not clamor
against the reason. There every will subjects itself to
the will of God. There man is at peace with God and
at peace with himself. There Simon Magus does not
deceive,* the Pharisees do not show off their large
phylacteries,* the Jew does not murmur; there Linus
rejoices at Peter's good as much as at his own. There
love is mutual, where all men feel affection for one
another. There discord does not disrupt affection,
and deceit makes no breach in it. There all things submit to prayer; nothing wars against affection. There
the deed keeps company with the will, and the deed
does not belie the affection.

No-one may attain this peace unless he has first
ordained peace in his spirit, unless he has first
quieted the tumult inside himself, unless he has first
cast out of himself the strife of fleshly thoughts,
unless he has first come to be his own master.

This threefold peace we have spoken of was
prefigured long ago by various signs. By the rest
which the children of Israel enjoyed in the Promised
Land is signified temporal peace, for, just as that
peace was strewn with various adversities, so temporal peace is upset by many setbacks. Through the
solemn Sabbath of the old law* is signified the peace
of our conscience, for just as on the sabbath day men
take holiday from servile work, so in peace of heart
they take holiday from slavery to sin. Through that
peace in which God rested on the seventh day from
his labor* is signified eternal peace, in which there is
rest from all labor.

The first peace must be trodden underfoot, the
second held fast, and the third sought out. If Cain
had had peace in his heart, he would not have set
upon his brother.* If Absalom had had peace of

Ex 20:10

Gn 2:2

Gn 4:8

2 S 15

Mt 27:3-5

mind, he would not have set upon his father.* If a tranquillity of conscience had calmed the spirit of Judas, he would not have fallen into the pit.*

O on what a secure throne is he set, who is soothed by tranquillity of mind! How comfortably does he stretch out on his bed, who arrays his spirit with peace! In this particularly should a man rest until he dies; as he progresses towards it, let him sleep and take his rest.

CHAPTER XXIII: ON PRUDENCE

*Mt 10:16
**Ws 7:30
†Si 14:22

Pr 15:18

*See Major,
(Ch.III,n.3)
p. 5 & PL
72-23 C.

discretio

[158]

If anyone desires to learn about prudence, let him proceed in this way: 'Be wise as serpents and harmless as doves'.* Again: 'Wisdom conquers evil.'** Elsewhere 'Blessed is the man who dwells on wisdom'.† Again: 'The foolish man stirs up quarrels, but the wise man quietens them'.* Seneca says: 'Anyone who desires to pursue prudence begins to live a good life, led by reason, and rates the worth of things not on the basis of mere reputation, but according to their own nature.'*

Prudence is the ability to judge* between good and evil things, and to judge of each, in the avoidance of evil and the choice of good. It is said, 'of each', for it is not enough to separate good and evil from each other, but one must also separate the many goods and evils from each other, and, among the goods, tell the better from the lesser goods, and among evils, the worst from the less bad. It is not enough to tell them apart, unless the good choice is followed and the evil avoided. Prudence teaches which things seem to be good and are not, and which do not seem good, but are.

O man, prudence teaches you that you should not

admire the transitory things you possess, nor esteem
great what is perishable. Prudence will teach you that
you may prudently dispense with those things which
you possess, which are not your own, and you may
profitably part with those things which you cannot
hold onto for ever. If you embrace prudence, and
persist in doing so, you will not suffer loss in anything, and, according as the changeableness of affairs
or times demands, so you will adapt yourself to time,
place, person, cause; nor will you change yourself in
response to any of them, but rather adapt yourself in
all things—just as the hand is the same hand whether
it is extended palm-open or clenched into a fist.[1]
Prudence neither wishes to deceive, nor can it
be deceived.

Prudence praises sparingly, and blames even more
sparingly, for too much praise is as reprehensible as
too much blame. The one is close to idolatry; the
other smacks of spite. Prudence does not bear false
witness to the truth for the sake of friendship. It
promises with discretion; it fulfils its promise quickly,
and does more than it has promised. Prudence is exercised at three times: it orders the present, foresees
what is to come, and recollects the past. For he who
thinks nothing of what has happened in the past loses
his life. He who does not think ahead about the
future, tumbles into everything unprepared. The
prudent man sets before his spirit both the evil to
come, and the good, that he may endure the one and
moderate the other. He is not always active, but by a

---

1.   The image of the fist and the palm is to be found in Cassiodorus,
PL 70:1157, and in Isidore *Etymologies* 2:23:1. It derives from a gesture of Zeno the Stoic, who used the device to demonstrate the difference between rhetoric and dialectic, rhetoric being like an open
palm and dialectic like a closed fist. Cassiodorus' source as a lost
work of Varro. Cicero also mentions the device in *Orator* 32:113.

quiet moment now and then refreshes his spirit. Rest
itself is filled with the study of wisdom and with
thoughts of good. For the prudent person never lan-
guishes in leisure, and never grows sluggish with laziness, but sometimes his spirit takes rest. He is never
slack, but hastens to complete what is delayed, settles
difficulties, makes light of what is hard, and tackles
demanding tasks.

The authority of a speaker does not move a wise
man, nor does a highly-wrought style, nor does he
think about what he may say or do, nor about how
much but rather what kind of good he may do. He
chooses and seeks what can be chosen in front of
everyone. Nor does he take up a higher place which
he must either tremble to stand in or trip in coming
down from.

He gives himself wholesome advice, whenever
prosperity of life or worldly honor beckons him,
and then he keeps his footing as if in slippery mud.
Nor does he allow himself to proceed impetuously,
but with a cautious step. To prudence belong circumspection and caution. Prudence weighs the future
according to the past, as, if a prudent man sees anyone
fall into such a vice, on such an occasion, he weighs
the future by this, so he will not fall into a like sin on
a like occasion. O how great a prudence it is to weigh
[159]   the future by the past, the present moment by what
has been done before, like by like, consequences
from signs!

To the same prudence belongs circumspection,
which is nothing else but precaution against the
opposing vices; by this means we avoid one vice in
such a way that we do not go rushing into its opposite.
For example, if we beware of avarice, let us not rush
into prodigality. Solomon urges us to this virtue,
Pr 4:23   saying: 'With all diligence, guard your heart'.* Being

about to say 'diligence', he prefaced it with 'all', in case, even if you bolt one door, you throw open the gate to others. For there are many who so avoid the attack of one vice that they slacken the tether on another. The vices give aid and comfort to one another, so that while someone gives one of them a wide berth, another vice gives the fugitive shelter in its own place.

To the same prudence belongs caution, by which prudence discerns the vices which display themselves in the guise of virtues. For this reason, Isidore says: 'The vices display themselves in the guise of virtues and thus they deceive their followers the more dangerously, because they hide themselves under the veil of virtue'.* Under the pretext of justice, atrocities are perpetrated, and lazy slothfulness is taken for gentleness. What is believed to be kindly done, is done out of the negligence of sloth.

Sententiae II: 35:1; PL 83:636

From all this, it is clear that the prudent man is content to live a good life. Thus Chrysippus says: 'The wise man lacks for nothing for he has within himself the highest good, and thus it profits him nothing to seek instruments of good outside himself'.* Within his mind he honors the Highest Good; he cherishes the whole within him, for he does not embrace merely its form outwardly. Anyone who seeks outside himself any part of the good, begins to be subject to fortune. But the prudent man possesses all his goods within himself, and if he loses all the good to chance, he will cry: 'All my possessions are within me, that is prudence, justice, fortitude, temperance.'* All those things which can be snatched away he considers not as goods. To the imprudent, nothing is enough; he is not content; nothing ought to remain his. Even if he needs nothing, he knows

Seneca, Ep. 13-15. Cf. Horace, Ep. 1. iii. 46, Satura 1. iii. 127.

Seneca, Ep.9:18

how to use nothing, and so he lacks everything.

[2] Prudence is the queen of the other cardinal
virtues. In her they find their principle; from her
they demand a measure; without her, what seems a
virtue melts into silliness, and what appears to be
good slides into rashness. Prudence teaches us what
we must think, what we must do, with what intention, and how we must carry it through to the end. It
measures human strength, sets boundaries to thoughts,
directs the movements of the mind, the insight of the
reason. It weighs the good and examines the evil. Of
what use is religion, unless it receives the seasoning of
prudence? What use is fasting, unless it is seasoned
with the salt of wisdom? Wherefore, O man, before
you tackle anything, look in the mirror of prudence
to discover how to perform your deed; read in the
book of prudence what must be done and what
avoided. That book does not deceive, or betray anyone, but all its opinions are true and honest statements.

CHAPTER XXIV: ON FORTITUDE

These authorities teach a man fortitude: 'Be brave
in war and do battle with the ancient serpent'.* Seneca
says: 'If you are greathearted, you will never consider
that you have been insulted. You will say of your
enemy, "He has not injured me, although he had a
mind to injure me.".'* O how generous is the
magnanimity which judges—when it has the oppor-

*Antiphon for
second Vespers,
Common of
Many Martyrs.*

**See Major, pp. 4-5,
PL 72:25A*

2.   This passage would appear to belong to this chapter, although
it is found at the end of Chapter Twenty-Four *On Fortitude* in many
manuscripts. In the PL it occurs in column 161 AB.

tunity to wreak vengeance—that it has already taken its revenge. Such a man considers it the highest and most honorable kind of vengeance to put the matter out of his mind. He attacks no-one from ambush, but proceeds against him openly. He does not begin a conflict unless he has declared his intention. Reverses do not make him downcast, nor do successes elate him. The brave man does not seek out dangers as the imprudent does, nor does he fear danger like the coward. It is fortitude which made Vincent* able to bear more while being tortured than the torturer himself could.

*of Saragossa, martyr [160]

O man, if you will embrace this virtue, you will not fear fortune's arrows; you will deride her flattery, and despise her anger. He who is brave is free; he is not a slave to fortune, or to the changeableness of the world. See how great was the fortitude of the martyrs, who overcame torments, who mocked the very tyrants in their greatness of heart. Although driven out of their bodies, they were not driven out of their minds; they did not turn their backs on their enemies, but magnanimously resisted them.

There is a threefold fortitude: the fortitude of the whitewashed hypocrite; the fortitude of the philosopher; the fortitude of the righteous man. The first chases a vain glory, but in the chase it deserves the ignominy of eternal damnation. This kind so drags down glory that it may not come to glory. It is rather idiocy than magnanimity, rather weakness than health. To this the heretics pretend, and this the false brothers affect.

The second is that fortitude by which philosophers despise worldly fortune. They deride glory, reject riches, forswear human power. But this fortitude was not sufficient for merit, and had no power to win the prize of life, for it lacked the principle—that is charity, which is the principle of all good affection.

According to this fortitude it is said that Cato had a stiff upper lip, Socrates had great-heartedness, and Diogenes contempt for the world. But because this fortitude did not have the foundation of faith, hope did not raise it, love did not perfect it, and it lost the merit of virtue.

The fortitude of the just man makes God its end; it does not fail to meet its obligations. This is the fortitude which despises death, opens its home to spiritual poverty, and forces pleasures to lie bound under the bridle of reason.

There are three kinds of misfortune: poverty, disease, the violence of a tyrant. Against poverty fortitude is strong, so that the spirit may not be broken, but grow greater within, and the more it expands in the mind, the less does it abound in the things of fortune. Fortitude is strong against the assault of disease, for in this sorrow it gives thanks to God, and finds spiritual delights in trouble, that the disease may bring greater benefit to the mind than harm to the body. And so disease brings medicine; weakness, health; sadness, joy. Fortitude outmatches the violence of the tyrant, from whose cruelty it draws the sting; it spurns prison and has no fear of death.

O man, your activities avail nothing unless they are strengthened by the pillars of fortitude. The building of good activities wobbles unless it is undergirded by the pillar of fortitude. If that is broken, the whole building collapses, and Samson, that is, the *Jg 16:29-30* strong man, kills himself.* Fortitude equalizes adversity and prosperity, and prosperity and adversity, so that no-one may be more elated in prosperity than *[161]* he is downcast by misfortunes. He considers prosperity as smoke and as a transient froth, misfortunes as a passing cloud. Great-heartedness itself demonstrates

[See XXIII, note 2]

that weakness makes a man strong in trouble, for trouble in itself has no virtue.

CHAPTER XXV: ON TEMPERANCE AND MODERATION

Ph 4:5

*Tt 2:12
†Tt 2:5-6

Ep 125:7

Source unknown
Source unknown

Ovid, Metamorphoses *2:137.*

Let the preacher proceed in this way in his sermon on temperance or moderation: 'Let your moderation be known to all men; the Lord is at hand'.* Again, the Apostle: 'Let us live soberly, righteously and piously in this world'.* Again: 'Being soberminded'.† And Jerome says: 'Moderate and temperate eating is good for the body and for the soul'.* Again: 'All things provided are subject to the virtue of continence'.* St Gregory: 'The purity of the continent is exhaltation of mind'.* Elsewhere, the poet says: 'The blessed keep to a middle way', and: 'You will go most safely down the middle'.*

Consider how much nature demands, not how much gluttony desires. If you behave with restraint, you will in that way arrive at a state where you are content in yourself. For he who is sufficient to himself is born to delights. Set a bridle on lust. Put away all the things which beckon to your spirit with blandishments and pleasure. Eat until you are not quite full; cease to drink short of drunkenness. Satisfy your desires with a little—for you should ensure that they cease to clamor. Do not sit down to eat to indulge yourself; let hunger whet your appetite, not the flavors. Let poverty never be sordid to you, or parsimony mean, or simplicity undervalued, or lightness wearisome. Do not admire the things of others, nor weep over your own. If you love continence, avoid what is vile before it ruins you.

Keep your words not sharp but mild; be yourself a fugitive from vice, and do not pry curiously into the affairs of others, nor scold them sharply, but correct them without reproof, so that you prevent hilarity by admonition, and pardon error easily. Do not praise or blame a man immoderately. Be a silent listener. Be quick to reply to a question; yield easily to him who quarrels with you; and do not descend to insults and cursing. If you wish to be continent, watch the movements of both body and spirit, making sure they are not indecorous; do not scorn them because they are hidden; it does not matter if no-one sees them, if you yourself see them. Be the familiar friend of few, but equable with everyone. Let your life-style be more secure than your face shows. Be merciful in punishment, a hater of violence, one who desires a good reputation, yet not one who sows the seeds of vainglory. Rather be one who hides his virtues from vainglory, as others conceal their vices; be a despiser of vainglory and of honors. Do not be harsh in exacting what is due to you.

'O how rare a bird on the earth is a white bird in the likeness of a crow',* which keeps the measure of the middle way. O how glorious is the virtue of temperance, which makes it a virtue to keep to a middle way, lest there be any sliding into a lesser state or swelling into an overabundance. This is the spiritual circumcision which cuts away the excess of each of the senses with the rasp of reason. To it Seneca invites us, saying: 'Let your life be moderated between good and publicly acceptable behavior. It is a great man who employs earthenware vessels as if they were silver; nor is he a lesser man who uses silver as if it were pottery'.* Again, he says: 'Let your dwelling be neither too humble nor too magnificent; virtue lies in moderation, not in grovelling'.* O man, tie yourself

[162]

Juvenal, Sat. *6:165, cf.* Anticlaudianus *1:241.*

Ep. *5:5-6*

Ep. *5:3*

to the bounds of temperance. Be careful neither to be
greedy, nor dishonorably to reduce your customary
liberality. And measure other virtues, too, by the rule
of temperance. In justice temperance must so obtain
that respect for its discipline may not grow cheap
because it is commonly despised. On the other hand,
do not allow the grace of human kindness to be lost
in savage retribution. This sets a measure upon fortitude so one may know both how to accept prosperity

Ph 4:12   and how to avoid ill-advisedly seeking misfortunes.*
This governs prudence, that it should not taste more
than it ought, but it should have a taste for sobriety,
and not grow vilely useless by pressing beyond the
proper limit of its inquiry.

In all things temperance adorns the substance of
good by its activities and gives appropriate shape to
its circumstances. It so measures times, places, persons and causes that, walking within its bounds, a
man cannot suffer ruin in the sudden losses of this
world, nor in the unexpected shocks of earthly life.
If a man is armed with this, nothing can goad him to
rage or prompt him to slander. The devil finds nothing
in him of which he may accuse him, his conscience
nothing to root out, the world nothing to deride, the
fire of purgatory nothing to purge.

CHAPTER XXVI: AGAINST LOQUACIOUSNESS AND WAGGING TONGUES

If anyone endeavors to beware of loquaciousness
and the unbridled wagging of the tongue, let him
pay careful attention to what follows. The Apostle

1 Tm 4:7   says: 'Avoid profane and old wives' tales'.* Jerome

Source unknown.

[163]
1 Co 15:33

Enchr. 163a

Ad Nepot. Ep.
52:15
Source unknown.

says: 'Let scurrility and wantonness have no place in your presence'.* Everything which does not edify the hearer is twisted into a danger to the listener: 'For gossip corrupts good behavior'.* Sixtus, too, says, 'An evil-speaking tongue is an indication of an evil mind'.* Your tongue follows your meaning; a word spoken without meaning is reprehensible. Augustine, too, says to Nepotianus: 'Let it be your duty, most dearly-beloved, to keep not only your eyes chaste, but also your tongue. Let your body never be moved to dissipation, nor your tongue to jests or empty words'.* Sixtus also says: 'Empty speech is an indication of an empty conscience'.* Whatever speech comes forth, such is the nature of the spirit proved to be.

O man, what will lie ahead for you in deeds, if you are found ungoverned in speech? It is not a greater glory to say memorable things than to bite back unprofitable ones. It is a foolish man who does not first test his word against the bounds of reason, before letting it trip off his tongue. A man should first subject each word to careful examination, before he says it aloud. Beware lest you speak words in public and your talkativeness causes embarrassment to those who are not learned, and offence to those who are learned. A flood of words signifies an inconstant spirit. Talkativeness paints on a man's face the nature of his mind.* Talkativeness changes a man into a buffoon, transforms him into a mimic, reduces him to a jester, lowers the dignity of human nature. The tongue must be bridled; as James says: 'It sets on fire the wheel of our birth'.* For the wheel of our birth is this present life, which, from our earliest years, revolves in a whirl of words. In adolescence, this mobility of the tongue burns to jest, in the grown man to deceive, in the old man, to slander. This spark must be put out, lest it burst into flame. This young shoot [must

Cf. Jerome,
Ep. 65

Jm 3:6

be destroyed], lest it grow into a forest. This trickle [must be stopped], lest it swell into a rushing torrent.

It is a greater matter to bridle the tongue than to capture a castle, for the one involves an attack upon the outside, but the other upon the inside man. The one takes up arms against you out of your very self; in the other case, the object of strife is something outside yourself. Yet it is at once the highest shame and the lowest despair not to be able to bridle this member; it is vile not to be able to bring your own servant into subjection. If the tongue is set in a slick place [i.e. the mouth] it is fixed there by perseverance; if it wishes to come out, let it be held back by moderation; let the bolt of reason be applied to the door, and the fence of discretion put round it. If a bridle is put on a horse so that it does not run away with its rider—where only physical danger threatens—how much the more is a bridle to be put on the tongue, through which danger threatens the soul? True simplicity is better than abundant talkativeness. Holy inarticulateness* is better than sinful eloquence. He who, without being asked, often gives way to garrulousness, is quickly condemned. Accustom your tongue, then, to speak well. Precious is the tongue which knows only how to form words concerning divine matters; holy is the mouth from which heavenly speeches always come. Consider how you are to render account for 'every idle word'.* As Gregory puts it: 'That which lacks either the profitableness of uprightness or the reason of a just necessity'.* Loquacity is the seed which bears no fruit, salt without savor which flavors nothing, but rather makes the earth infertile; it rouses listeners to roars of laughter.

O man, do not strive for many words, but for a fruitful brevity of expression, for, as Jerome says,

rusticitas—*implies an awkwardness in manipulating language.*

Mt 12:26

[164]
Source unknown.

striving to be brief, you ought not to speak at length.
If you have chastity in your mind you will not foul it
with dishonorable talk. 'Show yourself wise, not in
running about, and chattering, but in silence and sit-
Source unknown. ting still.'* The garrulous man never blushes to
speak; he does not consider what, but how much,
he may say; he measures the fulness not of his
opinions but of his words.

Moderate speech is holy and reverent; immoderate
speech is known for its immodesties. Certain men, in
order to indulge their talkativeness, ignorantly expound Scripture without understanding it. And when
they persuade others, they assume to themselves the
appearance of superior learning. The garrulous are
PL: infatnant surely to be avoided like poisonous beasts, who fool*
others with their own verbosity, and unwisely pour
forth what will benefit neither themselves nor others.
And, as Jerome says: 'Certain men carry most vile
rumors and say that they have heard from others what
Source unknown. has in fact come from their own lips'.* Some prate and
chatter against others, while about themselves they
are tongue-tied and dumb. Talkativeness is a mirror of
the mind and a garrulous tongue the writing of the
heart. Hear what the Gospel says: 'A good man brings
forth good things from the good treasure of his
Mt 12:35 heart'.* Solomon also says: 'In much speaking sin will
not be absent, and he who controls his lips is a very
Pr 10:19 prudent man'.* 'He who sets a guard on his lips preserves his soul, but he who is heedless will suffer
Pr 13:3 destruction'.* The wise man will be silent until the
right moment, but the lustful, the imprudent, the
bold, do not wait for the right moment. David says:
'The tongue-wagging shall not be raised upon the
Ps 140:9 earth'.* And Gregory: 'A tongue-wagging man is
ignorant; the wise man speaks little. Short speech adds
Source unknown. to knowledge; to speak much is foolishness'.* At first,

listen; be the last to speak. The last word has the
greater honor. It is better to have the last word than
the first.

CHAPTER XXVII: AGAINST LYING

Let anyone who wishes to avoid the bane of lying,
instruct himself by means of these sentences: It is said

Mt 19:18

in the Gospel: 'Do not bear false witness'.* And Paul
says: 'Putting away lies, let everyone speak the truth

Eph 4:25

to his neighbor'.* Solomon, too, says: 'He who lies

Pr 12:17

bears witness that he is a deceiver'.* 'The lying mouth

Ws 1:11

slays the soul.'* And David says: 'You will destroy

Ps 5:6
[165]
Source unknown

those who speak lies'.* Isidore, too, says: 'Everything
which is out of harmony with the truth is iniquity'.*

O man, how out of harmony you are with the
Highest Truth, when you act by the fictions of lying!
How do you think you will come to the Truth, if by
your words you dissent from the truth? I do not know
in what conscience anyone prays to God with that
tongue which has choked out a lie. There is no sin by
which the conscience is so branded, and with the mark
of falsehood. Although every mortal sin makes a man
a stranger to the truth, no evil does this more than the
lie, which denies the very nature of truth. This is the
vice which, having prepared false evidence, begets
flatteries, discovers deceits, indulges in slanders. By
this vice one speaks once in the heart and once in the
mouth and is divided within oneself. He denies with
his mouth what he believes in his heart. Through this
vice, the heart speaks against the heart, the mouth
goes against the heart. This vice gives rise to heresy;
it creates schisms, generates suspicions, raises
unheard-of rumors, white-washes shame, covers
what should be laid bare, lays bare what should be

veiled. It is present in perjuries, and in dishonest deeds; it works against all things which are in natural law to the benefit of neighbors, for it does battle with truth itself. It contains within itself the rot of an evil so great that it cannot be excused for any reason. Natural piety does not absolve the midwives from this guilt,* nor reasonable fear the Gideonites,† nor any trick of the mind Peter,* nor provision for Ananias' needs.*

*Ex 1:15-21
†Jos 9:3-6
Mt 26:70

Ac 5:1-6

There is no sin which so aspires to defraud, tends to deceive, looks to mislead, pants to betray, as the vice of lying, the disgrace of falsehood. 'O sons of men, how long will you love vanity and seek after falsehood with leaden hearts?'* You are too willing to follow after the vanity of our nature, if you also bend the truth in words. But if the fault were only in lying, punishment will come in truth, in the future, and he who is now false through lying will in the future be truly in Hell.

Ps 4:3

You know that through lying you imitate the devil, the father of lies,* who did not stand in the truth, but fell through the vanity of pride. Those who back away from the truth are his sons. Those who indulge in falsehoods are his accomplices. O man, if there is falsehood in your lie, there will be truth in its punishment. O wretched outcome of lies, which from a false premise infers a true punishment!* O what imprudence, what folly, to bear the blows of eternal punishment for a lying word! How does he who is besmirched with the filth of a lie err from the proper duty of the tongue! A man sufficiently expresses the wheel of his birth* when he slips through the offence of falsehood. O man, if you wish to avoid lying words, teach your tongue the truth, and turn it from scurrility. Lying is servitude, which taints all speech with its own bitterness.

Jn 8:44

A reference to the study of dialectic.

Jm 3:6

There are three kinds of lie: the lie of vanity, the lie of deceit, and the lie of intention. Of the first it is said: 'Everyone speaks vanity to his neighbor'.* Of the second it is said: 'Every man is a liar'.* Of the third: 'You will destroy all who speak lies'.* The first is wretched, the second blameworthy, the third an abomination. The first is a matter for punishment, the second for blame, the third of malice. The first is spontaneous, the second is premeditated, the third elaborated.

Ps 12:3 [166]
Ps 116:11
Ps 5:7

CHAPTER XXVIII: AGAINST SLANDER

These authorities afford a remedy against slander. Jerome says: 'When a deed is the invention of some-one's slander, the reputation of another is damaged.'* Again, he says: 'You cannot justly reprehend in others what you yourself do, nor can you argue that something is merely pretence, when you yourself are held guilty'. Again: 'Beware of having prurient ears or a prurient tongue, that is, of either slandering others, or listening to slanderers'. 'Slander no-one, nor think yourself holy in that respect, if you tear others to pieces, and if you wound others by your slanders; this is not to make them mend their ways, but to satisfy your own vice'.* Again: 'It is incongruous to cover the body, and to let the tongue wander loose in the world'.* See that while you reprehend vices, you do not fall into the vice of slander. And so: fault-finding is a kind of slave; however much slaves are given, it is too little for them; nor do they consider what is given, but how much, and they are consoled in their discontent only by slander.* Again: 'He who often slanders others offends many. It is base to tear to pieces those who

Source unknown.

Source unknown.

Isidore, Synon. on detraction; *PL 83:857.*
**Source unknown.*

The text at this point is corrupt.

are not present, and to speak ill of a stranger's life. Anyone who excuses himself by someone else's mistake is not very skilful in putting his case'.*

The slanderer carries the likeness of a scorpion, for just as the scorpion presents a young girl's face, but carries a sting in its tail, and deals blows from above with its curved tail, so the slanderer utters pleasant words to men's faces, and hides in secret the sting of slander. Inflicting the wound as if from a higher position, he slanders his betters.

O man, what do you think of yourself, when you brandish the spear of slander? The first arrow is turned back upon you, and the wound is dealt to you rather than to others. You ill hide the enormity of your deed if you desire to cover it by slandering others. While you slander men, you render yourself suspect, make yourself hateful to everyone, and those whom you ought to befriend with honest speech, you strive to turn by slander's venom into enemies. While you work at painting others black, you stain yourself even deeper. And what you say falsely of others, you find true of yourself. Of slan-

Ps 5:11

derers it is said: 'Their throat is an open sepulchre'.* This sepulchre, whitewashed outside, contains within the corpse's stench; so the slanderer, wishing to whitewash his inner malice, lets it spew out by the gateway of slander. But instead, by this means the sepulchre is opened, and the stench of the inner corruption comes out. Slanderers are like hounds who rashly rush after barking dogs and bite them all. These

Terence, Andria
5.4.38

are they who find a difficulty where there is none,* a spot in something spotless, angularity in something round, shadows in something bright. This is the plague of hypocrites, the bite of the envious. This plague

[167]

spares nothing, increases blame, diminishes grace, errs against its neighbor, sins against the Holy Spirit.

Lk 12:15,
Mt 3:22

Jn 8:48

Inspired by this evil plague the mocking Scribes and
Pharisees said: 'By Beelzebub the prince of devils he
casts out devils'.* And others cried: 'You are a Samaritan and you have a devil'.*

O man, what is the good of slander? What profit
lies in the evil-speaking tooth? While you think to injure your neighbor, you rather increase his honor. For
the distemper of envy, accustomed to speak ill of the
good, also does violence to virtue. The evil-speaking
tongue demeans itself to vent malice in vices, and
arms itself completely to diminish the righteousness
of its neighbor; it so polishes another's reputation
with the rust of its slanders, that by its own gnawing
it rubs clean and exalts another's glory. Slander
publicizes enmity, and lays bare a maliciousness of
spirit and, through slander something unsuspected
within spews out poison.

O man, if you argue, do it according to measure;
reprehend with caution, not to cause your neighbor
to stumble, but so he may be corrected. Argue, not
to cover up your own villainy, but to heal another's
wounds. Slander belongs to sycophants, who fawn to
swindle money, who slander to move the rich to give
generously, and who with flatteries play sweet music
in the ears of the powerful. According to the gifts of
the table, they weigh out their praises. They acquire
through slanderings what they cannot get by virtuous
means. The tongue of these who chase food will be
food for everlasting flames, and as it attracts gifts by
slander, it will be torn apart by punishment in hell.

Slander is the enemy of the mother of virtue, that
is love, which he drives from himself who beats his
neighbor black and blue with slander, for the Holy
Spirit flees from a whisper of slander, detests the
reproving lie, the sin of slander. Neither now nor in
the future life will he who offends the Holy Spirit

find much forgiveness.

O man, you who are dust and ashes, with what effrontery and flushed with what a supercilious countenance of coyness, do you dare to spew forth the poison of slander against your better, or to bring a judge's sentence against him who is less evil, even if only a little? If you judge your neighbor unjustly, you will be judged justly by One greater, and you will experience the judgement of eternal damnation for your slanderous judgement.

CHAPTER XXIX: EXHORTATION TO PRAYER

This is instruction in prayer: 'Everything you ask in prayer, believing, you shall receive'.* 'Pray for each other, that you may be saved, for the heartfelt prayer of a righteous man has great power'.* 'The Lord is far from the wicked, but he hears the prayers of the righteous'.* 'Prepare your soul before praying, and do not be like the man who tempts the Lord'.* 'God hears the prayers of the injured'.*

Mt 21:22

Jm 5:17

Pr 15:29

Si 18:23

Si 35:16

Son, do not despise yourself in your infirmity, but pray to God, and he will heal you. Rise from your bed; turn from your transgression, and set your hands to work. Take time by night and by day to pray and to read, and when sleep has fallen from your eyes, then let your senses awaken to prayer.

[168]

Just as it does not befit soldiers to go out to war without arms, so it does not benefit the Christian to set out without prayer. Whence Jerome says: 'Let prayer arm a man as he goes out of his lodging'.* The harder we are pressed by the tumult of carnal thoughts, the more ardently we should stress our

Ep. 22:37

prayers. It is better to pray in silence of heart than with words alone, without the insight of the mind. For sadness of the heart is consoled by the profitableness of singing psalms.

Such should be a man's feeling in praying to God, that he should not despair of his prayer being granted. We pray in vain if we do not have the confidence of hope. He who has turned away from God's precepts does not deserve what he asks in prayer. Caesarius said: 'We should devote ourselves to prayer and reading in such a way that we can pray even when we are carrying out some task with our hands at the same time'.* Just as wormwood and even pigments drive away poisonous creatures, so wholesome prayer drives out evil thoughts. Do not deform prayer, O man, in any circumstances. Seek the eternal, not the temporal. If you ask for earthly things, your prayer lacks substance; if it does not arise from love, it lacks form. Ask therefore piously, so that prayer may be well formed; ask with perseverance, that your intention may be firmly rooted. Ask for those things which look to eternal salvation, that they may cling to a solid foundation.

Source unknown. Cf. RB 48

Do not ask for immoderate things, lest your prayer be turned to sin, like that of Judas. Do not ask out of a grudging spirit, like the sons of Zebedee, who asked Christ that fire might come down from heaven to devastate the Samaritans.* For they did not ask out of an insight into justice, but out of a love of vengeance. If you pray, exclude from your spirit the tumult of thoughts; close the door of your mind, and enter into the chamber of your heart.* When you pray to God, preserve the sweetness of your ointment, lest dying flies destroy the sweetness of the holy oil.* That is, beware lest bad thoughts mingle themselves with your prayer, and take away the value of the

Lk 9:54

Mt 6:6, Cf. Anselm, Prologion I.

Qo 10:1

prayer. If you offer God the sacrifice of prayer, drive
away like Abraham the birds of prey from the sacri-

Gn 15:11 fice,* lest they set upon the offerings and kill them.
For one should be careful lest unclean thoughts corrupt
the sweetness of the prayer which is sent up.

There are many, who have God in their mouths and
the devil in their minds, who praise God with their voices
but blaspheme in their minds, and although their
tongue is singing hymns, their spirit is in the stewpot.
What they vow with their mouths, they disavow in
their spirit. Such—as far as they are able—mock God,
blaspheme against his divine majesty and, when they
pray with their tongues for sins to be forgiven, do not
doubt in their minds that they will continue in them.
Further, there are those who defile their lips with
prayer, and kill their souls. Of these Seneca says:
'Now how great is the madness of men! They whisper

[169] ugly vows to God. If they have no audience they fall
silent. What they do not wish men to know, they tell
to God. So live among men, as if God beheld you; so

Ep. 10:5 speak to God as though men were listening to you'.*
O man, if you wish to be heard, ask worthily for
worthy things, and beg God for what it suits God
to give.

For there is a certain kind of prayer full of dangers, by which we ask for evil things. Such was the
prayer of Judas the betrayer, for he asked for the
betrayal of the Saviour. Another kind is self-seeking;
by it we ask for temporal things; such was the prayer
of the sons of Zebedee, in which they asked that one
might sit on the right hand and the other on the left
of God in his kingdom, which they believed would be

Mt 20:20-3 ruled like a temporal kingdom.* Another is fruitless—
in which one who perseveres in sin asks eternal salvation. Of this it is said: 'Not everyone who says to Me

Mt 7:21 "Lord, Lord" shall enter the kingdom of heaven.'*

Mk 11:23-4,
Jm 16:23.

A play on
numen—nomen

[169]

Sg 3:6, cf. BS 25

Another kind is fruitful, in which nothing appropriate is omitted. Of this it is said: 'Whatever you ask of the Father in my name, he shall give you'.* Where is the deity of the name understood better than in the name of the deity?* He truly asks in Jesus' name who asks with the purpose of being saved and asks for eternal salvation. This prayer alone pleads before the Judge, declaims before the Prince of Heaven. It is said of the bridegroom in the Song of love, on this subject: 'Who is this who comes up out of the wilderness like a column of smoke, perfumed with myrrh and frankincense, and with all the powders of the spicemerchant'.* The [prayer] truly ascends which pierces paradise, and goes up to the very throne of God. This is exquisitely called a column and straight, for just as a rod is raised up straight on high, so a fruitful prayer does not turn back upon earthly things, but is directed inflexibly towards heavenly. Yet it is exquisitely compared with smoke, for just as smoke born of fire tends upwards, so a fruitful prayer, arising from the furnace of love, ascends on high. It is exquisitely said, too, that it goes up 'out of the wilderness', for the spirit by which such prayer is poured out is set apart from all the strife of evil thoughts. It is: 'perfumed with myrrh and frankincense'. Frankincense has a scent, myrrh bitterness. By frankincense, therefore, is meant devotion of the mind; by myrrh the bitterness of repentance. Therefore the ointment of prayer should be compounded from the bitterness of repentance for our sins, and the fragrance of inner devotion. Anyone who wishes to pray fruitfully must repent of his sins, and his prayer should be fragrant with devotion of the mind. 'And with all the powders of the spicemerchant'. The spicemerchant is Christ, who adorns his own with various spices of the virtues, and makes them

drunk, as if with spiced honey. All the powder of this
spicemerchant is manifold virtue, from which we
should compound the ointment of our prayer.

CHAPTER XXX: ON REMORSE OR CONTRITION

[170]

*JI 2:13
*the Baptist
*Mt 3:2
Ps 51:19

Source unknown

Source unknown.

affectus

By these authorities can one learn remorse and
contrition of heart: the prophet says: 'Rend your
hearts and not your garments'.* And John*: 'Repent,
for the kingdom of heaven is at hand!'* The psalmist:
'The sacrifice to God is a contrite spirit'.* The holy
Augustine, on the same subject: 'He who lacks remorse
does not offer pure prayer'.* And the holy Isidore:
'The sins we have committed must first be purged
with tears, and then thoroughly cleansed with acu-
men of mind, before we contemplate what we
desire'.*

Remorse of heart is humbling of mind with tears
for the remembrance of past sin, with love for the
Judge and with fear of the judgement. That act of
remorse is the more perfect which casts out of a
man all affections leading to carnal desire, and fixes
its purpose, with wholehearted application of mind,
on the contemplation of God. The soul of the elect
is affected by remorse in twin ways: that is, while
he thinks of the evils of his own deeds, and while he
sighs with desire for eternal life.

There are four states of affection by which the
mind of the righteous man is wholesomely stricken
with remorse. The first is the memory of past deeds.
The second is the consideration of his pilgrimage in
this life. The third is the remembrance of his own
sins. The fourth is the desire for his heavenly home,

and how he may be able to arrive there more quickly.

The tears of penitence are reckoned before God as baptism. Love your tears, and the more you were given to fault, so much the more be prone to lamentation. Great sins require loud lamentations. But he is blessed who feels remorse agreeable to God. Remorse is health of soul; remorse is the forgiveness of sins. Remorse is the first* plank after a shipwreck. It is the first medicine in the cure of sin. Remorse is a spiritual washing of inner rebirth, without which adult baptism avails nothing. Without this the body is subject to the Judgement of Christ; without this, confession is fruitless; without this satisfaction is vain. This is the water purging the mind, making fertile the purpose, watering confession, quenching the soul.

This is the water which drowns the Egyptians, that is, which blots out the first stirrings [of sin]. This is the spiritual flood which destroys all flesh, that is, which blots out every carnal thought. But it is a three-fold washing: of baptism, of repentance, and of martyrdom. The first is the baptism of those who make a beginning, the second of those who are returning, the third of those who win through. Of the first it is said: 'Wash yourselves: be clean'.* Of the second it is said: 'Wash me more thoroughly clean of my iniquity'.* Of the third it is said: 'They washed their robes in the blood of the Lamb'.* The first washing is symbolized by the sprinkling with living water which was performed in the Old Testament; the second by sprinkling with ashes; and the third by the blood of the red heifer.* For what is living water but baptism? What is the sprinkling of ashes but the humility of remorse, through which man shows himself to be dust and sits in sackcloth and ashes? What is the blood of the red heifer but martyrdom, red with blood, which draws its efficacy from the passion of

culpa

lit. secunda

Is 1:16

Ps 51:4

Rv 7:14

Nb 19:2

[171]

Christ? This baptism is threefold: the baptism of the
river, which is in water; the baptism of fire, which is
through penitence by the grace of the Holy Spirit;
the baptism of blood, which takes place in the com-
bat of martyrdom. Through the first, a man is garbed
in the first robe; through the second, the torn robe is
mended. In the third, the second [robe] is made
ready. In the first, the old man is destroyed; in the
second, the inner man is renewed; in the third, the
flesh dies. The first affects everyone, the second,
many, the third, a few.

O happy bath of repentance, which cleanses the
human heart as often as necessary. This is the herb of
the heavenly Fuller,* which cleanses of squalor the
soiled garments of those who are his own. This is the
heavenly soda which, coming down in the dew of
divine grace and boiled by the sun of righteousness,
rubs away the spots of sin. This is the bubbling lye
composed of the ashes of humility and the water of
repentance, with which the head of the inner man,
that is, the mind, is washed clean of the worms of the
vices. In the face of ruin this is men's only solace,
which in the place of Christ's passion, provides a
remedy against sin, so that Christ is not forced to die
as many times as man sinks into the abyss of sin. This
is the spiritual circumcision which is performed with
the stone, Christ, and by it the foreskin of the flesh
is cut away—that is, the desire for carnal uncleanness.
If you are shipwrecked in the abyss of sin, cling to the
plank of contrition, which survives the shipwreck,
and brings a man to harbor.

Enter your own conscience; examine it. First consider the state of your own prudence. If it seems to
you that it has turned inward through desire; if the
throat [has erred] through gluttony, the ear in hearing
debilitating melody or by willingly listening to evil-

*Teasel. Cf. Ad
fratres in eremo;
PL 40: 1253-5.*

speaking, if the tongue has halted in word, the sense
of smell erred in sweet smelling, the sense of touch in
theft, or if your steps have gone astray in a level place;
if in any or in all of these you discover sin, wash it
away through the act of remorse. According to the
extent of filthiness, measure the amount of the washing; according to the severity of sickness, measure out
the quantity of medicine. According to the aberration
of the fault, weigh the course of punishment.

Poenitentia, punire   Repentance is so called from 'punishment';* the fault
is blotted out which is punished by rubbing it out.
Fear indeed is the mother and source of repentance;
it conceives repentance and brings forth contrition.
Whence Isaiah says: 'In thy fear, Lord, we have
conceived, and we have brought forth the spirit of
Is 26:17-18   salvation'.* Repentance, then, is to weep for sins
previously committed, and, weeping, not to commit
[sin again]. For he who weeps for some sins and
meanwhile commits others, either does not yet know
how, or merely pretends, to repent. What does it
profit anyone if, for example, he weeps for sins of
dissipation, and still sighs with surges of greed? Isidore says: 'He is a mocker and not a penitent who
Sent. II.xvi;   goes on doing what he repents of'.* Nor does he seem
PL 83:619.   obediently to entreat God but arrogantly to mock
him. 'A dog returning to his vomit'* is the penitent
Pr 26:11 [172]   returning to his sin. Many weep without ceasing, and
do not cease sinning. I notice that some people take
tears for repentance, and I perceive that they have
not the affection of repentance, for they pour
out their tears not in remembrance of their sins, but
through righteousness of mind; and immediately they
[In one group of   commit with renewed habit those things which they
manuscripts, the   have wept for again and again.*
work ends here.]

CHAPTER XXXI: ON THE CONFESSION OF SINS

Jm 5:16

Authorities: 'Confess your sins to one another'.*
And elsewhere: 'I will confess my transgressions to

Ps 32:5

the Lord'.* Job also says: 'I shall speak in the bitter-

Jb 10:1

ness of my soul'.* In the bitterness of his soul speaks
he who confesses his sin aloud according to the contrition of his heart. The Apostle too says: 'He who
believes in his heart for righteousness sake, will con-

Rm 10:10

fess with his lips for salvation's sake'.*

It is ordained in the Old Testament that a man

Lv 14:2, cf.
Misc. 14.

healed of leprosy should show himself to the priest.*
By this it is made clear that the patient healed of
spiritual leprosy through contrition is bound to show
himself to the priest in confession. Therefore, confess
your sins that you may be absolved; accuse yourself
that you may be excused. If you are not now your
own accuser, you will have three accusers on the Day
of Judgement: God, accuser and judge; your conscience, accuser and punisher; the devil, accuser and
avenger.

This is the difference between the judge upon

soli et poli

earth and in heaven*: he who accuses himself before
an earthly judge is found guilty, but he who confesses
his sin before the heavenly Judge is forgiven. Before
the earthly judge repairing and removing the crime
takes precedence, the accused [man] who refuses to
acknowledge his crime, or who imputes it to another,
may in some sense be excused. But before the heavenly Judge, he who calls his crime his own, and does
not impute it to another, nor ascribe the cause of his
crime to fortune or to fate, is forgiven.

Confession can be fourfold: that is, confession which is extorted, the confession of desperation, confession of repentance, and confession of praise. Confession when it is extorted results from some sort of constraint, such as when the devil confessed the Son of God. They said: 'Jesus, Son of the Living God, why have you come to destroy us before it is time?'* Confession in desperation is that by which Judas confessed, saying: 'I have sinned in that I betrayed righteous blood.* And Cain: 'Greater is my iniquity than I can deserve to be forgiven'.* Confession of repentance is that which proceeds from penitence, of which James says: 'Confess your sins to one another'.* Confession of praise is that in which we acknowledge the goodness of God, saying: 'We confess the Lord, for he is good'.* By this, too, did Christ confess, saying: 'Father, God of Heaven and earth, I confess you'.*

The confession of sin, however, is twofold—sometimes general, sometimes particular. General is that made in the morning and evening office, that is, the confession of venial and hidden sins. Special [confession] is that made for mortal and manifest sins. The clergy are obliged to make confession every Sunday; the laity are bound to make special confession three times in the year, that is, at Christmas, Easter, and Pentecost.* This is symbolized in the Old Law, in which the children of Israel were commanded to offer themselves to the Lord at Jerusalem three times in the year, without fail. Thus we, too, are commanded to offer ourselves to God through confession in the spiritual Jerusalem—that is, the Church—three times in the year, and without failing in good works.

But this has fallen into disuse nowadays, when layman or clerk confesses scarcely once in the year, and when he does confess, it is to be feared that he

Mt 8:29

Mt 27:4

Gn 4:13

Jm 5:16

Ps 136:1

Mt 11:25

[173]

The Fourth Lateran Council (1215) ruled that confession was obligatory once a year.

confesses rather in order to satisfy custom than out of a contrite spirit. Negligence holds certain men back from confession; shame some, bad habit others, still others the fear of the penance to be imposed, others again the intention of continuing in their crime. These are the frogs which, thrust into the mouth of a dog, make him dumb.* By some it is asserted that this is the green frog which dwells in reeds, which, if it is thrust into a dog's mouth, makes him dumb. The dog is the unclean sinner, whose barking, or the sound of his confession, is taken away by the plagues of which we have spoken, as if they were frogs thrust into the dog's mouth. These are the foreigners who had filled in the well of Abraham.* By 'the well of Abraham' is meant confession, from which the faithful soul draws water springing up into everlasting life. This well the aforementioned plagues stop up, lest a man draw up the water of salvation from the well of confession. This is the reservoir of Bethlehem, to which the Philistines laid siege, from which David desired to drink.* For David signifies the faithful soul, who desires the water of confession and salvation. But the troops of the Philistines, that is, the multitude of the aforementioned pest, lay siege to it, and prevent the faithful soul from drawing water.

Confession should be all-encompassing and not particular, so that a confession may be made of known sins specifically, but of unknown sins in general. For it is the nature of pious minds to find fault where there is no fault, and to acknowledge it to be there through confession, where it is not evident through admission. Just as forgiveness is all-encompassing, so too confession should encompass all, for the grace of the Holy Spirit knows nothing of belated endeavor. Him whom he heals, he heals completely.

Isidore, Etym. *12:6:58-9.*

Gn 26:15

2 S 23:15

Three things should come together so that confession may be true confession: that is, contrition of heart, profession of the mouth, satisfaction in deed. Therefore, if any of these is lacking, it is not confession, but so much vain opening of the mouth. For confession is a complex thing, known by three signs. This is the road of three days [journey], along which we should go in solitude, that is, we should tend toward our heavenly home that we may worship our God.

CHAPTER XXXII: OF REPENTANCE OR SATISFACTION

Mt 3:8
Mt 3:2
Jb 42:6
[174]

Ps 51:6

'Bring forth fruit worthy of repentance'.* Elsewhere: 'Repent, for the kingdom of heaven is at hand'.* Job says: 'I repent in dust and ashes'.* Outward repentance had its beginning from Christ, through preaching, from Job its example through satisfaction, from David through teaching and instruction. He says: 'Against you alone have I sinned',* and so forth.

But the fruits of repentance are remedies: prayers, fasting, the singing of psalms, vigils, oblations, reading, almsgiving, stringent habits. Against the disease of dissipation, prayers and fastings are the medicine: prayers, that God may put out the fire of lust with the dew of heavenly grace; fasting that may chastise the beast of our flesh. 'This kind of devil is not cast

Mt 17:20

out except by prayer and fasting.'* The singing of psalms and reading are effective against the sin of listlessness; they should arouse the spirit from torpor, teach it to abandon idleness and to pursue serious things. Almsgiving, too, provides a remedy against

Cf. Bernard, Asspt 5; SBOp 5:255.

avarice, abstention against drunkenness. For, as Gregory bears witness: 'Opposites cure opposites'.*

The seven chief virtues must be set against the
seven principal vices: against pride, humility; against
envy, love; against anger, longsuffering patience;
against listlessness, cheerfulness of mind; against
avarice, generosity; against drunkenness, sobriety;
against dissipation, chastity.

Just as we sin in three ways, so we should repent
in three ways. Because we sin in thought, let us against
this sickness bring the remedy of contrition. Because
[we sin] with our mouth, let us bring to bear the
antidote of confession. Because by deed, let us set
against this the remedy of reparation.

Repentance, however, is two-fold. One kind is
momentary and transient, the other, persevering and
long-lasting. The first is insufficient to blot out sin;
the second sufficient for the forgiveness of sins. The
first is incomplete, the second complete. Of the first
says Isidore: 'He is a mocker and not a penitent who
continues in the sins he has repented'.* Of perseverance
it is said that repentance should come to an end only
with death. The sinner should offer through repentance as many burnt-sacrifices of satisfaction of his
own for himself as he has offered vices of his own
to the devil, that our flesh, which before bore the
thorns and thistles of vices, may be ploughed up by
penitence to bring forth an increase of the virtues.
And, just as we must always have the eradication of
our sins in mind, so penitence must remember, that
repentance may give rise to remembrance, and
remembrance cause sorrow. In this purgative fire one
should be stationed in this present time, lest he be
mortally racked in the flames of hell.

There is a three-fold fire: purgative, probative, and
destructive. Purgative fire is satisfaction; the probative
is temptation; the destructive is eternal damnation.
Of the first it is said: 'He will baptize us by spirit and

Sent. II.xvi;
PL 83:619

Mt 3:11
*Ps 17:3
**Mt 25:41

by fire'.* Of the second it is said: 'You have tested us by fire'.* Of the third: 'Go into eternal fire'.** But the fire of purgatory is twofold: one kind lies on the way, that is, repentance; the other after life, that is, in purgative punishment. If we are purged in the first, we are free of the second and third. If we do not experience the first, we shall feel the second, or

[175]

even—what is worse—the fire of destruction. The first purgatorial fire shuts out the second, that is, the second purgatory and eternal destruction. For the first purgatorial [fire] is like the sketch and shadow of the second, for, just as the sketch and shadow of a physical fire causes no pain, but physical fire itself causes agony or burning, so the fire of repentance has no bitterness by comparison with the second purgatory. For, as Augustine says, the punishment of

Source unknown.

purgatory is much worse than any earthly punishment.*

Ez 33:11

Hb 12:6

O man, the patience of God invites you to repentance, his power to fear, his kindness to love. Consider how great is his power to punish, how great is his patience towards the penitent! Behold, how holy is he who gives you time to repent! He does not wish for the death of the sinner, but that he may turn back and live.* And this proceeds wholly from his gentleness and love. For the Father 'chastises every son whom he receives'* or loves.

CHAPTER XXXIII: ON ALMSGIVING

Is 58:7
Lk 11:41
Lk 6:30

'Break your bread with the hungry, and take the needy and the wanderer into your house.'* Elsewhere: 'Give alms, and everything will be clean to you'.* Again: 'Give to all who ask of you'.* And: 'Blessed is

Source unknown.

Source unknown.

the man who rescues him who is about to perish'.*
Again: 'If you see someone perishing of hunger and
you do not help him, you have slain him'.*

O man, almsgiving is the seasoning of fasting, the
ornament of prayer, the embellishment of vigils, the
ensign of generosity, and the especial remedy of sin.
To this Christ invites you, by example dispensing

reading pauperibus
for PL pauperis.

everything to the poor,* by word preaching works of
mercy. Do not excuse yourself from it on grounds
of poverty. If you cannot give money, give a crust of
bread; if you cannot do that, at least give a drink of
cold water. If you cannot help your neighbor by your
actions, help him by your words, either by interced-
ing for him, or by instructing him. For almsgiving has
many aspects: from the hand, in generosity to the

*Reading egestanti
*with MS Vesp.0.
xiii, f. 66, for PL*
eroganti.

poor; from duty, in ministering to the needy;* from
the tongue, in teaching your neighbor, or in inter-
ceding for him; from the spirit, in suffering with the
sinner, or in pardoning injuries.

Certain alms are prescribed; some are voluntary.
Those are prescribed which arise from circumstances;
those are voluntary which are independent of circumstances. These are the circumstances of almsgiving:
who, what, how much, to whom, where, when, and

Cf. Jerome, Comm.
in Ep. ad Ephes.;
PL 26:546A.

why. *Who:* whether [the giver is] a rich man or a poor
man, for the almsgiving of the poor is more pleasing
than that of the rich. For this reason, the Lord says
in the Gospel that the poor woman who cast two
mites into the treasury had given more than the rich

Mk 12:43

who sent large amounts.* By 'who' we are also to
understand whether [the giver] is just or unjust. If an
unjust man gives alms, it serves him to wipe out
punishment, not to deserve glory, but if a just man
gives alms, it serves for both. By *what* is hinted that
alms should be given of one's own property, not of
another's. Almsgiving out of what has been stolen

or plundered is not right, for, as the authority says: 'To give alms from the substance of the poor: that is like slaughtering a son before his father's eyes'.* By *how much* we are shown that we should not give everything to one person, but a number of separate gifts should be made to a number of persons. By *to whom* it is indicated that alms should be lavished on the poor rather than on the rich, and rather on kin or close relatives than on a stranger, rather on members of the household of faith than on the perverse. Thus, to suggest *how much* and *to whom*, it has been said: 'He has been generous; he has given to the poor'.* *Where* means in the open, to the edification of others, yet not so as to win human praise. For this reason the Lord says: 'So let your good works shine before men that they may glorify your Father who is in heaven'.* *When*—at the time of need; *why*—at the prompting of God, not for earthly gain or human favor. Almsgiving is the dew of heaven, putting out the furnace of sin. This alone pleads before God; this alone will plead for you before the severe Judge. For what will the blessed be praised by Christ in judgement? For keeping silence? No. For continence? Not at all. For keeping vigil? In no way. But because they gave alms.

Almsgiving is like the oil, fasting like the lamp. For just as when the oil is taken away, the lamp goes out, so fasting without alms is devoid of virtue. That specific and natural precept which says: 'What you wish men to do unto you, you should do to them' argues against the man who denies alms to the needy.

There is a three-fold almsgiving: cold, lukewarm, and hot. It is cold when done, not out of the instinct of natural piety, or the fervor of love, but only [to win] human favor. It is lukewarm when done out of the instinct of natural piety, such as occurs among infidels at the prompting of natural affection. It is hot, however,

Si 34:24
[176]

Ps 112:9

Mt 5:16

when performed in the ardor of love. The first deserves punishment; the second avoids it; the third prefigures glory.

Alms should be given not only out of our own excess, but out of what we ourselves need. It is said: 'He who has two tunics, let him give one to him who has none'.* The tunic is specified, not the cloak, for the tunic is the more necessary. This indicates that we are bound to give not only what we do not need, but also from what we do. This was made clear in the story of the blessed confessor Martin,* who gave to the poor part of the cloak which was his only covering, on a bitter day.* There are some who bestow on the poor things they would scarcely cast before swine, by which they think their sins will be redeemed. And this is like a blasphemy against God, to honor the rich with unworthy things, and to offer heavenly pearls to swine to tread upon.

Lk 3:11

of Tours.

*Sulpicius Severus,
Vita S. Martini;
PL 20:159-76.

CHAPTER XXXIV: ON FASTING

The prophet admonishes penitents to fast with weeping and wailing.* And the Lord says: 'When you fast, do not be sad-faced, like the hypocrites.'* Gregory also says that the sinner should engage in fasts, so that in time God may turn his heart to repentance.* Fasting chastises the flesh, uplifts the spirit, bridles burgeoning desire, alerts the reason. By fasting, Moses deserved to speak with God,* Daniel to interpret dreams,* Elijah [was worthy] of succour,** the Ninevites of the remission of sins.* Christ gave us an example of fasting, when he fasted in the wilderness for forty days and nights.*

But physical fasting is not profitable without

Jl 2:12
Mt 6:16

Cf. Moralia VI.33;
PL 75:973-4.

Ex 20
[177]*Dn 7:8*
**1 K 17-19*
Jon 3

Mt 4:2

mental fasting; otherwise, it is deceitful and misleading. For of what value is it if the mouth fasts from food while the tongue gorges itself with lies, the eye feasts on vanities, the ears relish stories, and the nose lazes among sweet fragrances, the sense of touch runs about on smooth surfaces, the hands are snatching, and the foot wanders from its proper path? Let the other senses fast with that of taste, so that they who were companions in pleasure may become fellows in suffering.

Fasting has many faces: there is the fasting of habit which is not performed out of love, but only out of habit, so that a man should not seem to sail against the common practice. That is profitable only in that it avoids setting a bad example and gives no offence. There is a fasting of avarice and greed, where the stomach is kept empty so that the purse may be kept full, and that is self-defeating. There is the fasting of sickness kept so that health may follow; that is neither good nor evil, but [morally] neutral. There is the fasting of drunkenness and gluttony so that the sated appetite may regain its edge, and that is the worst of all. There is fasting for the sake of praise and outward appearance, which hypocrites perform, so that they may win human praise; that, too, is evil. There is fasting from want or necessity, by which the poor fast, and that is neutral. There is fasting by obligation which many religious perform, and that is not sufficient. Leaving aside the other fasts, we must aspire to that which comes of charity, by which the body is chastised, the spirit rules, and thus man lives like an angel. By fasting a man becomes spirit, by moderate eating a man, by excessive, a beast.

There are many circumstances of fasting, which are the principle of fasting itself: that is: from which, where, when, and why. *From which:* one should

abstain from delicious food. What profit is it for him
to fast from food if what he loses in time [spent
eating] he makes up for in enjoyment or in quantity? At meal-times someone fasting should eat
moderately, so he may give part of his portion to his
neighbor; and he should so deny himself that he may
benefit his neighbor. We must also consider *where;*
the custom of the country must be followed, so:
'When in Rome, do as the Romans do'. For this
reason, Augustine says: 'When I am in Rome, I do not

Source unknown. fast on Saturdays; when I am in Milan, I do'.* *When:*
fasting should take place on the appointed days. For
there are certain days when we must not fast, as on
Sundays and certain great festivals, because it would
give offence. *Why:* let it be at the prompting of God,
and of charity.

As many as the kinds of carnal abstinence, so many
are the different kinds of fasting. There is fasting in
continence, in abstinence, in humility, in modesty, in
exultation. Of fasting, Augustine says: 'Let fasting sing

Source unknown. your praises, not a belching belly.'*
[178]
Fasting provides good medicine for body and soul.
It preserves the body from sickness and the soul from
sin. In this medicine, heavenly philosophy accords
with natural [philosophy]. This medicine purges the
stomach from the ill-effects of drunkenness, and the
soul from unworthiness. If in Paradise Adam had
fasted from the forbidden fruit, he would not have

Gn 3:23 been condemned to exile.* If Esau had fasted from
Gn 25:34 lentils, he would not have lost his birthright.* If Noah
had fasted from wine, he would not have uncovered his

Gn 9:21 thighs and his shameful parts.* Therefore, through
fasting, the body is cleansed to receive the Eucharist
sacramentally, the spirit to receive it spiritually. This
should be the preparation for taking the Eucharist.
Therefore, let a man despise material food in the

present time, lest in the future he feel the fire of hell.

Let three things make up fasting: good intention, generosity in almsgiving, the kindling of charity. If the flesh yearns for the delights of food, let a man remember that he would only fill himself with matter for dung. If the flesh wishes to anticipate the hour of eating, let it take refuge in exercise, lest leisure awaken greed and increase appetite. O man, if you consider the Fathers of old, who used to take food twice, or only once in the week, your fasts will seem to you as nothing, or very moderate. But if the examples of past generations do not move you, at least let the infancy of the blessed Nicholas* move you, who for four or six days at a time ceased to suck the breasts. Let it shame a grown man not to fast, when he sees how a little child fasted. The example of a little child throws us into confusion, when infants and children correct us.

On the legend of St Nicholas, see Misc. 2.

CHAPTER XXXV: INSTRUCTION IN WATCHFULNESS

'Blessed is that servant whom the Lord, when he comes, shall find watchful.'* Again: 'If the head of that household had known at what hour the thief would come, he would have watched'.* Again: 'Watch, therefore, for you know not at what hour your Lord will come'.* Again: 'Watch and pray, so that you may not enter into temptation'.* Solomon says: 'They who are watchful in the morning shall find me'.*

Mt 24:46

Ibid. 43

Ibid. 42
Mt 26:41
Pr 8:34

Christ invites us to watchfulness by example, in spending the night in prayer, and in watching out for our instruction. Bodily vigils are to be performed to exercise the body, and to drive away torpor, to escape

the phantoms of the night, to avoid the slippery
passions of the flesh, so as to make a place for prayer
and to deny the Enemy entry.

The faithful soul should, like a man of great
Sg 3:7, cf. Misc. *10* strength, 'Guard the bed of Solomon',* and grasp
his sword poised [in readiness] across his knees in the
face of the terrors of the night. Not only in material
vigils, but also in spiritual, the faithful soul should be
watchful on behalf of the Church of God, the bed
of Solomon—that is, of Christ—on which he rested, for
Pr 8:31 it was a delight to him to be among the sons of men.*
He should also grasp his drawn sword, that is, he
should wield the sword of discretion, to restrain the
[179] stirrings of the flesh and the attacks of the devil
which are the most to be feared and avoided in the
darkness of this world. We must undertake spiritual
vigils, rather than bodily ones, so that the mind of
each person may be watchful over his flock, that is
the stirrings of the spirit, lest the wolf—that is, the
devil—lying in wait, should force any stirring out of
its proper place. We should be watchful lest the thief
—that is, the devil—enter into the cloister of our heart
through dissipation, or into the chamber of the mind
through idleness, and steal the tapestries of the soul,
that is, the adornment of the virtues. This thief is
sometimes an invisible robber, when he does violence
through the tyranny of princes; sometimes the thief
makes his entry through heresy: now he comes like a
bird, flying high in pride, now like a snake, when he
deceives through dissipation, now like a lion, when
he carries on by open violence, now like a serpent,
through hidden temptation.

There are four parts of the sin of the night-hours.
Cf. Amalarius of The first is called midnight, when a person delights in
Metz, Ord. evil-thinking; the second, the late evening, when men
Antiph. 5. —that is, reasonable urges— lie as prisoners to a misled

will; the third, cock-crow, when the will clamors into action; the fourth, predawn, when the deed is openly performed. Night vigils were not instituted without reason, for by them it is signified that we must rise in the middle of the night to sing the night office, so that the night may not pass without divine praise and so that bodily vigil may awaken spiritual.

Let it shame a man if the sun rise before his own vigils, and if the cock crow at night, while he himself is absent from divine praise. O man, beware the watchman's stick, lest he find you sleeping; beware of the robber, lest he suffocate you loitering. The watchful rod, or the rod of vigilance, is the rod by which, once it has been brought into the house, the thief tests to see whether the head of the household is asleep or the household drowsy. If the head of the household sleeps, he steals everything he finds. If he is awake, he flees. In a spiritual sense, the rod of vigilance is Christ, of whom Jeremiah says: 'I see the rod of vigilance'.* He it is who tests by his own judgement whether the head of the household is asleep, that is, whether a man's own continence is sluggish. If he finds him sleeping, he condemns him; if watchful, he finds in him no reason for injury. Likewise, the devil, who is the spiritual thief, if he finds a man watchful, flees; if sleeping, he snatches away everything. Because Ishbaal slept in the middle of the day, he was slain by the robbers.* Samson, napping, was captured by his enemies.* Sisera, asleep was slain by a woman.** Gideon slew his sleeping enemies.* Christ just before his Passion reproached his sleeping disciples.*

Jr 1:11

2 S 4:5
*Jg 16:21
**Jg 4:21
Jg 7:19
Mt 26:40

CHAPTER XXXVI: EXHORTATION
TO LEARNING*

Cf. Misc. *16*

So learn as though you were to live forever. So live
as though you were about to die. On the same subject,
the Apostle says: 'Read books and carry books with
you'.* Seneca says: 'Life without letters is death and
the tomb of the living man'.* Jerome: 'My head was
already sprinkled with grey hairs, but it did not see
the end of zeal for learning'.* And elsewhere: 'I
would rather learn from others with diffidence, than
rashly pour forth my own opinions'.*

*A misquotation
of 2 T 4:13.
*Cf. Ep. 82:3

*Source unknown.

[180] *Source
unknown.

Reading sharpens perception, adds new dimensions
of understanding, kindles an ardent desire to learn,
affords fluency, warms the lukewarm enthusiasm of
the mind, casts out sluggishness, tears away the web
of lust, excites groans of heart, coaxes forth tears,
brings us close to God. Ovid writing on love says: 'If
you indulge yourself in leisure, the arrows of Cupid
will destroy you'.* If you read, idleness flees, the devil
finds you occupied. Go into the wine cellar,* in which
love is ordained: that is, read Scripture, inquire into
its meanings. In this cellar, a man becomes drunk in
such a way that he comes away more sober still.

*Remedia amoris
139.
*Sg 2:4

When you read a great deal, set one thing in particular before you, chew over one very pithy thought,
that the more firmly it takes its root in your spirit,
the more it may please the palate of your mind. If
you set out upon any reading, do not pass over it in a
moment, but dwell upon it, not passing on to something else as though you found it distasteful. For, as
Seneca says: 'A plant which is often transplanted does
not grow well, and a medicine often changed does not

Cf. Ep. *2:3*   penetrate to the heart of the wound'.* And if at some
time it should come about that you are given the
books of earthly philosophy to read instead of books
of theology, look out as you go along to see whether
in them you may perhaps discover something which
may instruct you in good behavior, something which
is in harmony with the catholic faith—so that the
Hebrews may be enriched by the spoils of Egypt, and
gold may be borrowed from the Egyptians to be used
in building the tabernacle, and their wood in building
the Temple. Hiram, King of Tyre, gave generously of

1 K 5:9   his wealth,* and the children of Israel drank from the
well of the Amorites; with his own sword was the

1 S 17:51   enmity of Goliath checked.* So, then, should we pass
through foreign camps to be explorers and pilgrims,
not men who belong there.

O man, read so that you understand, make an
effort so that you read, for, as the moral philosopher says: 'To read and not to understand is to be

Source unknown.   negligent'.* Consider the words of Papilianus the
philosopher, who says: 'If I now had one foot in the

Source unknown.   grave, I should still wish to be learning'.* Nor should
an older man disdain to learn from a younger, for
sometimes something is revealed to younger men,
which is not [revealed] to their elders. The Apostle
says: 'If something is revealed to a younger man, let

1 Co 14:30   the elder keep silence'.* Moses, skilled in all the learning of the Egyptians, did not scorn taking the advice

Ex 4:18-20   of Jethro the Gentile.* And Solomon, to whom was
given the treasure of wisdom, did not disdain to hear

2 Ch 9   the wisdom of the Queen of the South.* For water
runs down through stone channels into the spice
gardens. Plato, a Gentile, went down into Egypt so
that he might read the Book of Genesis, suffering
many storms on the way. Shall the Christian spurn it
when it is before him, and ready to hand to instruct

him? For clerks of our own day follow more readily
the schools of Antichrist than Christ, are rather given
to gluttony than glosses; they collect pounds rather
than read books, they understand Martha better than
Mary, prefer to read Solomon rather than Solomon.[1]
Now all learning goes cheap, all reading is half-hearted;
there is no-one who reads books: 'There is not even
one; all fall off, and all alike are made unprofitable'.*
Now the school of Christ is deserted; it is concerned
with two things, with life and with learning, but the
true life is despised, and learning is buried. Once,
even though the good life was not loved, yet learning
was embraced. But now exorbitance, obstinacy, and
alienation are at their height, when not only good
behavior is set aside, but also what befits it, that is
learning, is despised.

Ps 14:1
[181]

If by chance anyone does learn, he does not make
God his end, but earthly gain or human favor. He does
not seek Christ in his reading but money; the earth,
not heaven. Such men deflower virgins, that is, they
corrupt the virgin sciences, because they prostitute
them for gain and, so far as they can, they destroy
them. What is worse, and more monstrous than every
monstrosity, they make their listeners pay to hear
theology; learned men sell it so that they may expound
their knowledge vaingloriously. Now venial theology is
prostituted, and waits to sell her favors like a harlot.

Once Masters were held in the highest honor, but
now they have a deserved reputation for being foolish
and fatuous. Now they do not ask what there is in the
storehouses of the mind, but what there is in the
coffers. Who are those who are held in honor?—the

---

1.   The entire sentence is a play on words: *gula—glossa; libras—libros,*
Martham—Mariam. The word which is intended to be paired with
Solomon (—*Salome,* perhaps) remains obscure.

rich. Who are those who are despised?—the learned.
Who are those who have a place in the palaces of
kings?—the moneyed. Who are those who are shut out
of their halls?—the lettered. Now the household of
Croesus is honored, and the household of Christ is
despised. How glorious it is to read, how fruitful to
scour the Scriptures, to gaze into the mind of God,
and to delve into his teaching! But a person should
read in a threefold book: the book of the creation,
that he may discover God; the book of conscience,
that he may recognize himself; the book of Scripture,
that he may love his neighbor.

CHAPTER XXXVII: ON HOSPITALITY

Heb 13:2

Paul says: 'Do not neglect to practise hospitality'.*
Peter, similarly: 'Be hospitable to one another without
1 P 4:9   grumbling'.* And Isaiah: 'Take wanderers and the
Is 58:7   needy into your house'.* Hence Truth says: 'I was a
Mt 25:35   sojourner and you took me in'.* O man, Christ in his
members cries at the gate and asks for hospitality.
Take in the pilgrim on earth, that he may receive you
rejoicing into the homeland. Abraham deserved to be
given his son, because he entertained angels in the
Gn 18:10   guise of sojourners.* Lot, because he took in angels as
if they were sojourners, deserved to be saved from the
Gn 19:15   destruction of Sodom.* The widow who in kindness of
hospitality honored Elijah deserved to have her son
1 K 17:22 restored to life.* The disciples going to Emmaus
were enlightened through the teaching of Christ, but
they deserved to be more fully and more perfectly
Lk 24:13-31 illuminated by him through the service of hospitality.*
O man, if you know yourself to be a stranger and
pilgrim in this world, if you recognize your own

condition of pilgrimage, do not refuse hospitality to
the pilgrim. For, if you shut out the poor man of
Christ from under your roof, you shut out Christ
himself from the guesthouse of your heart. Hear
what he himself says: 'What you have done for one
of the least of these my brothers, you have done for
Mt 25:40 [182] me'.* But hospitality should be joyful, munificent,
showing humility, displaying generosity. For a great
part of true hospitality is an unruffled countenance.
For this reason it is said: 'Above all, bear a happy
Ovid, Met. 8:677-8. face'.* Munificence, too, is a part of hospitality; we
should not respond reluctantly to someone asking
for food, but rather go beyond his request in carrying
out what he asks. For example, the guests of those
'going to Emmaus' must not only be invited, but
drawn in. The guests must be shown humility, too,
Var: humanity so that by the grace of humility,* which wholly fulfils the duty of hospitality, the service rendered may
be more generous than requisite.

Therefore let us receive as a pilgrim him who for
our sakes came to earth on pilgrimage, who for us left
his native land and set out on his way as a beggar.
O joyous hospitality which is shown to Christ in the
poor! O happy couch, on which Christ rests in the
body! O happy table, at which sits the Man [who is]
God in Man. O man, among the gentiles the laws of
hospitality are observed; among the faithful they are
broken. Brute beasts are glad at the coming of their
kind, and hold out in their way a law of sociability.
Men however hold back from the duty of humanity.
Is 23:4 'Blush, O Sidon, speaks the sea.'* Let the sea blush to
be assisted by the rivers; let the rational blush to be
instructed by the irrational. Let the sun blush to be
warmed by the hearth and by torches.

But just as the faithful soul is bound to show to
Christ in his members the duty of charity, so he is

bound to perform a spiritual service in his mind for
the Head himself, for Christ. Everyone should invite
Christ into the house of his mind with heartfelt cries
of welcome, and prepare a table for him in the house
of his mind with honest and wholesome thoughts, and
offer him the wine of love.

Thirdly, the faithful [soul] should also prepare
for Christ a guestchamber, as it were, so that he may
receive a heavenly viaticum, a spiritual Eucharist, the
body of the Lord. At the coming of such a guest, let
him cleanse the house of his own body, clear it of the
muck of dissipation, the dust of vainglory, the filth of
gluttony, that when he comes, he may be pleased to
rest there calmly, just as he says: 'I and my Father
Jn 14:23   will come and will make our home with him'.* Do
not let the filthiness of the lodging offend the eyes of
such a guest.

CHAPTER XXXVIII: THAT PREACHING SHOULD BE PERFORMED BY PRELATES

I have explained what preaching is, what form it
should take, and on what subjects it should be
delivered. It now remains to show who the preacher
should be. Preaching ought to be the work of prelates,
and sermons should be delivered by prelates. Two
things are their province: learning and living; learning,
so that they may instruct others; living, so that they
may set an example to others by living a good life. To
signify this, it is laid down that in sacrifices the crop
of the turtle-dove should be cast by the side of the
Lv 1:15   altar.* By the turtle-dove is symbolized the simplicity
of the preacher; by casting his crop to the side it is

understood that the preacher should perform by his
actions what he propounds by his voice. The same
thing is symbolized by the backward curve of the
pastoral staff: what he preaches to others, he ought to
apply back to himself, in the performance of good
works. To press home these two things—that is,
prudence, and a good life—it is said of the steward:
'Who do you think is the prudent and faithful
steward'.* For the preacher should be faithful in
word and deed: faithful in word, lest he mingle
falsehood with truth; faithful in word, lest he preach
the word with an eye on men's favor. He should be
faithful in word, lest he sell his preaching for earthly
wages; faithful in word, lest he contradict his words
by his deeds; for this reason it is said of false preachers:
'Our innkeepers mix wine with water'.* For they
mingle water with wine who preach the false with the
true, as the heretics do, and those who sell the word
for human favor, like the hypocrites, and those who
by preaching swindle their way to earthly goods, like
merchants, and those whose deeds belie their words,
like false Christians.

   [The preacher] should also be faithful in his
actions, so that what he does he may do with a right
intention, and that he may set God as the end of his
deeds. And so he should be wise in deed and in word.
In word, that he may know what things must be said
in preaching, and what must not. In deed, that he may
know to whom and when he must preach—that is, he
should preach on more important themes on more
important occasions and less difficult matters on less
important. To whom, in case he casts pearls before
swine to be trodden underfoot, or holy things of God
before the unworthy, as before the dogs.* When, that
as the occasion demands, he may expound the word;
when an opportune time is lacking, he may be silent.

[183]

Mt 25:23

Is 1:22

Mt 7:6

As Solomon says: 'There is a time to speak and a time

Qo 3:7   to be silent'.*

Preachers need knowledge, that they may be
thoroughly conversant with both Testaments, and
experienced in the weighing of texts,[1] fluent in words,
circumspect in all their deeds, despisers of the world,
conscientious in doing their duty. For Malachi says
of the prelate: 'The lips of the priest guard knowledge,
and [men] ask the law from his mouth, for he is a

Ml 2:7   messenger of the Lord of Hosts'.* And Jesus son of
Sirach says: 'If you have knowledge, answer your
neighbor; if not, let your hand be over your mouth,

Si 5:14   lest you are caught in making an ill-conceived remark'.*
For greatly to be feared is the gospel warning: 'If a

Mt 15:14, Lk 6:39   blind man leads a blind, both shall fall into a ditch'.*
And this apostolic warning: 'If a man is ignorant, let

1 Co 14:30   him be ignored'.* And what will the Lord say to the

Mt 25:12   foolish virgins? 'Verily I say to you, I do not know you'.*

Cf. Seneca, Ep.   And this one: the aged schoolboy is accursed.* Again,
36.4: senex   'The sinner a hundred years old will be accursed'.**
elementarius

***Is 65:20, cf.*   For there is a certain cultivated ignorance, when
Seneca, Ep. *36.4.*   someone is able to learn and chooses not to; this is
stupid and lazy and easily put right; therefore it is
inexcusable. Of this it is said: 'He did not desire to

Ps 36:4   understand so that he might do good'.* Again, 'Man,
when he was held in honor, did not understand, he is
to be compared with foolish beasts, and becomes like

Ps 49:21   them'.* This ignorance is characteristic of priests who
fall from contempt into ignorance, and out of pride
remain in foolishness. They are priests and prophets
without reason, teachers of impossibilities, guessing at

[184]   secrets. O vile ignorance, abominable folly, which

---

1.   Texts = *sententiae:* perhaps intended in the sense of the term in
Peter Lombard's *Sentences,* which formed the basis of theological
studies in the schools.

imposes silence upon the prelate, and makes our watchdog, that is the shepherd, mute; this is that frog which, when it is thrust into a dog's mouth,

Isidore, Etym.
XII.6.58-9.

silences his barking.* The prelates of our time seat themselves upon a throne before they are instructed beneath the birch: they don the robes of a Master before they undertake the hard work of the student. They choose to be eminent, not to be useful; the reward of honor, not the burden of hard work.[2] To such a prelate it can be said: 'Physician, heal your-

Lk 4:23

self'.*

Orator, plead for yourself; you who are a vicar of Christ, imitate his work, who 'Began to do and to

Ac 1:1

teach'.* He who teaches but does not do, defies Christ. He lays on those subject to him an unbearable burden, yet he is not willing to put out a finger to

Ac 1:1

move it.*[3]

Some hide in a handkerchief the talent of divine wisdom which has been committed to them—that is, those who, out of idleness, do not wish to preach. Some hide it in the dung-heap—that is, those who in their deeds contradict their own words; others hide it in the mud—those who hide the word out of envy.

---

2. A play on words: *praeesse, prodesse; pretium honoris, pondus oneris.*

3. Miller suggests that Alan means that only bishops have duty to preach, rather than the priesthood at large (p. 234, n 7). He also points out (p. 236, n. 10) that stupid ignorance, idle ignorance, and ignorance which can be remedied are distinguished in mediaeval theology as formal degrees of ignorance.

CHAPTER XXXIX: TO WHOM PREACH-ING SHOULD BE DELIVERED

Now that I have said by whom preaching should be given, and what kind of men preachers should be, it remains to show to whom preaching should be delivered—that is, to the faithful who desire to hear the word of God with a certain hunger of mind. Of them the Lord says: 'Lift up your eyes, and see how the fields even now are whitening ready for harvest'.* *Jn 4:35* The fields ripe for harvest are said to be the minds of men, made ready to accept the word of God. This is the good earth, which receives the seed and bears fruit. Preaching should be withheld from the unworthy and obstinate, for those who reject the word of God make themselves unworthy. Wherefore the apostles say to the Jews who reject their preaching: 'Because you have repudiated the word of God and proved yourselves unworthy of eternal life, see, we turn to the gentiles'.* *Ac 13:46* He who divulges secrets to the unworthy lessens the greatness of the secrets; and the vessels of the Lord are not to be set before the Babylonians.

It is better to speak to the young in parables, and reveal to adults the mysteries of the Kingdom of God. Little children must be fed with liquid food, grownups strengthened with solid food, in case the little child is made mortally ill by solid food, and the adult is revolted by liquid. Thus, each, severally, may receive what is appropriate to his position.

It is proper for the preacher to take up the position of an earthly physician or doctor. Just as an earthly physician varies the forms his remedies take according

to the different diseases he treats, so a preacher
should apply the remedies of admonition. Thus, if he
preaches to the dissipated, let him bring to bear texts
which speak against dissipation, and adduce appropriate reasoning; let him show that it is abominable
before God and man, how it reeks of infamy, reeks
in a man's own flesh, reeks before his neighbors and
reeks before God. Now let the preacher cut with the
knife by threatening; now let him apply the poultices
of consolation. In the same way let him dispute against
other vices, according to the way in which he sees his
listeners to be entangled by different vices.

[185]

Cf. 2 Co 8:9

cf. Jerome,
Ep. 52.4.

Mt 5:3

If he preaches to the poor, let him discourse on
poverty, commending it, and taking his example from
our head, Jesus Christ, who, when he was rich in
heaven, was made poor for us on earth, that, by his
poverty he might make us rich.* Let the Fathers of
old, too, come in as examples, those who, naked,
followed the naked Christ.* Let him show how the
blessed are the poor in spirit, not the rich in tax-
bracket.*

If he preaches to the rich, let him invite them to
give alms, to despise wealth, to love heavenly riches,
so that, if they abound in worldly riches, they may
not rest their hearts there; if they have wealth, let
them not solicit it, for to have wealth is a matter of
fortune, but to solicit it is a matter for blame.

Cf. Lk 3:14

If he preaches to soldiers, let him urge them to be
content with their own wages, and not to threaten
strangers; let them exact nothing by force, terrify
no-one with violence; let them be defenders of their
homeland, guardians of widows and orphans. So let
them bear the outward arms of the world that they
may be armed inwardly with the hauberk of faith.

If he speaks to public-speakers,[1] let him warn

---

1. *Oratores:* orators or legal advocates. The two skills fell into the
province of rhetoric in roman times. See chapter XLI below.

them, lest they support an unjust cause for gain or weaken a just case out of rancor and hatred, lest they sell their tongues, prostitute their wisdom, run after what is false, and venerate lies.

If he speak to the learned, let him warn them that they should teach as God prompts them, and that they should make God the end of their efforts; that they should not chase after the breath of popular favor, or earthly wages, that they should evince in deed what they set forth in speech.

If he directs his sermon to prelates, let him exhort them on the subject of the governance of their people, that he may encourage them with the hope of heaven, correct them with warnings, direct them with blandishments.

If he preaches to the princes of the earth, let [the preacher] warn them, that they should strive after prudence, loath avarice; that they should not abandon the path of justice, and that they should temper severity with clemency.

If he speaks to cloistered monks and religious, let him bring to bear for their instruction the examples of the Fathers of old, who led this present life in almost too great a castigation of the body. Let him show that it is worth little to begin, unless the beginning terminates in a worthy end, for no-one setting his hand to the plough and looking backwards is fit *Lk 9:62* for the kingdom of God.* And the wife of Lot, look-*Gn 19:26* ing backwards, was changed into a pillar of salt. *

If he delivers a sermon to married people, let him commend the state of marriage, faithfulness to the marriage-bed, the virtue of the sacrament. Let him show how marriage had its beginning in paradise, and how the Fathers of old deserved to attain eternal life in the married state.

If [he preaches] to widows, let him emphasize the

burdens of marriage—the care of children, making a
living, running a household—and how glorious it is
for those who have been tested, to avoid carnal indul-
gence, and to serve God in freedom!

If [he preaches] to virgins, let them be recom-
mended to cleanliness of body and purity of mind,
through which man rises above his humanity, over-
coming the flesh and behaving like the angels.

CHAPTER XL: TO SOLDIERS[1]

[186]

Lk 3:14

John the Baptist says to soldiers: 'Do violence to
no-one, and injure no-one. Be content with your
wages'.* Soldiers have an example for their own lives,
the blessed martyr Sebastian, himself a soldier, who
did earthly military service under the Emperor Dio-
cletian, but did not shrink from spiritual agony. He
rendered to Caesar what was Caesar's, and to God

*Mt 22:21, Mk
12:17
**of Marseilles
(tc. 290).
†an early martyr
of dubious
existence.

*The Desert
Fathers

what belonged to God.* [They have] the blessed
Victor,** too, blessed Hippolitus†, and many others
who served wholeheartedly as earthly soldiers, and
happily deserved to be promoted to the everlasting
army of the Highest King. The cohort of the thebaid,*
too, so wore the sword-belt of outward knighthood
that they inwardly fought devotedly for God. The
outward appearance of knighthood is the symbol of
an inner knighthood, without which the outward is
empty and vain.

*Lk 22:38, Cf. Ber-
nard, Csi 4.3.

But just as there are two parts of the man—the
bodily and the spiritual—so there are two swords*

---

1. For Alan, the word *miles* would have had the connotation of
knighthood; he would have seen the knight as—quite literally—the
soldier of Christ.

proper to repulse the various attacks made upon men:
the material sword, by which injuries are kept at bay,
and the spiritual, by which vexations of mind are kept
at bay. That is why it is said: 'Behold, here are two
Lk 22:38   swords'.* Let the soldier be girded outwardly to keep
the uneasy peace of the world, and also inwardly, with
the sword of the word of God, to preserve the peace
of his own heart. For this especially were soldiers
ordained that they should defend their native land,
and that they should repel the attacks of the violent
upon the Church; but now soldiers have been made
the leaders of pillaging bands; they have become
cattle-thieves. Now they engage not in soldiering,
but in plundering, and under the guise of soldiers,
they take on the cruel nature of marauders. Nor do
they fight against their enemies so much as victimize
the poor, and those whom they should guard
with the shield of knightly protection, they hound
with the sword of savagery. Nowadays, they prostitute
their knighthood, they fight for gain; they take up
arms to plunder. Nowadays they are not soldiers,
but thieves and robbers; not defenders but invaders.
Into the bosom of Mother Church they plunge their
swords, and the force which they should expend
against the enemy, they expend against their own
people. They cease to attack their enemies—either
out of idleness or out of cowardice—and against the
peaceful household of Christ they wreak havoc with
their swords. They deserve honorable service and
temporal largess, and they are not denied the pay-
ment of an eternal reward. While they are bound in
duty to exercise a bodily knighthood, all men are
bound by commandment to take up spiritual service.

The earthly knight lives in a camp, leaves behind
the embraces of his wife; is satisfied with meagre food;
keeps vigils, girt about with arms; he resists the enemy,

and takes care of his fellow-soldiers. Such should
every man be in spirit as is an earthly soldier in deed.
Of the soldier of Christ it is said: 'The life of man

Jb 7:1   upon earth is a soldier's service'.* Elsewhere: 'Here
Heb 13:14   we have no safe lodging'.* The same Apostle says
that we are guests and strangers here, but in the
future we shall be fellow-citizens with the saints and

Eph 2:19   members of the household of God.* The Christian
should live, therefore, during the pilgrimage of this
life, as if in a camp; let him not think he has a safe
lodging here, but let him await an everlasting habitation in heaven. Of these dwellings it is said: 'In my

Jn 14:2 [187]   Father's house there are many mansions'.* He
should live as though at the moment of death; he
should live in the tent of the flesh as though he were
about to leave it. Let him leave behind the embraces
of earthly pleasures, flee the flood of gluttony. Let
him be vigilant against the attacks of the spiritual
thief; let him be girt with spiritual arms and provided
with the hauberk of faith; let him be girt about with
the sword of the word of God; armed with the lance of
charity, let him put on the helmet of salvation. Armed
with these, let him contend against the three-fold
enemy: against the Devil, lest he seize him; against
the world, lest it reduce him; against the flesh, lest he
desire what is forbidden. Let him take care of his
fellow-knights, that is the faithful, in generosity, if
they are in need, in admonishings, if they stand in
need of them, in sharing the sorrows of the sick and
the joys of those who are well.

CHAPTER XLI: TO ORATORS, OR ADVOCATES

Ps 10:18
Is 1:17

Scripture says to orators: 'Do justice to the fatherless and the oppressed'.* And Isaiah: 'Help the oppressed and defend the widow'.* For the orator should be fortified with the truth, disposed to discretion, burning with charity, a despiser of avarice, a seeker after justice, lest either falsehood cloud his reason, or indiscretion diminish the truth of his words and hatred make him suspicious. Let greed not sway his spirit, nor injustice lead him into trackless places. Let not his tongue be hired out for money. Let him not win the breath of popular favor with witticisms, but let him bring his oration to a right end and have an honorable conclusion. Let him not prostitute his tongue, nor sell his discourse for a bribe, nor sell the gift of God, nor hire out for a fee the free gift of God. What he receives by the workings of grace alone, let him not abuse by selling. O how execrable is simony, to sell the heritage of the poor, to hire out the help of the helpless! Among almsgivers, he who advances the widow's cause does not hold the lowest place, for he not only defends but also assists her, if he protects her property by the force of his reason. Yet no-one's poverty or wretchedness should sway an advocate to falsehood, nor should anyone's prosperity demean him into behaving unjustly.

Truth always affords strength to reason, and gives weight to a speech which lacks it. He who does not take care to do right—when he is able to take care—is the same as he who gives assent to an injustice. For this is to visit the wretched in prison, to take up the defense of the oppressed. This is to clothe the naked, to take up the cause of the destitute for their support. This is to feed the hungry, to give drink to the thirsty, to dispense medicines to the sick, to receive the pilgrim, to take up him who is destitute of all help, to take up his cause to defend it. He who provides the needy with a defense, in a just cause performs the whole work of mercy.

Advocate, why do you fail to defend widows in their need? You do not lose anything in expounding your knowledge, nor forfeit profit through this generosity. This is that noble possession, which scorns a greedy possessor; when it is not used for the public good it slips away. And the spiritual orator, that is the just man whose prayer rises to God, should plead before God for the guilty, with pious prayers, so that even if damnation ought to be exacted according to the deserts of the guilty, yet, by gracious divine mercy, he may be given time for repentance and amendment of life. For: 'The heartfelt prayer of a righteous man has great power'.* The righteous man pleads for the guilty before the divine mercy, so that by grace the guilty may be freed from harm and pointed to salvation—since without divine mercy human weakness can be of no avail. And even if the prayer of the righteous does not always lead to the desired end in another, yet he who prays always comes to that end himself; if the sin of one for whom he prays is not forgiven, yet the prayer of him who prays is turned back upon himself. The doctor will not always cure, nor the orator always persuade, but if he omits nothing he is able to do in the circumstances, he has done his work.

[188]

Jm 5:17

CHAPTER XLII: TO PRINCES AND JUDGES

To the princes of the earth it is said: 'Love justice,
Ws 1:1 you who judge the earth'.* Elsewhere: 'And now,
O kings, understand and be instructed, you who
Ps 2:10 judge the earth'.* O princes of this world, you whom
the Lord has set over the heads of men, do not be
swollen with pride, blinded with greed, debauched
with cruelty. Consider the greater power set above
you, which will judge you in [the Day of] Judgement.
Even if a prince is surrounded by the pomp of his
household, if he is set upon a kingly throne, yet he
will not be able to stand against the will of God, for
Cf. Rm 9:19 who can resist God's power?* Therefore let every
prince humble himself beneath the powerful hand
of God. Nebuchadnezzar, because he did not
acknowledge the divine power over him, took on the
Dn 4:22,29 likeness of a beast; Manasseh, King of Israel, because
he did not acknowledge the divine power over him,
2 Ch 33, 2 K 21 fell victim to that power in his last captivity.*

O prince, if you wish to judge the earth rightly,
judge rightly the earth of your own body. For there
is a three-fold earth: the earth which we tread, the
earth which we live in, and the earth which we seek.
The earth we tread is the material earth, which is to
be trampled on; the earth which we live in is the
earth of our own body, which must be tended; the
earth which we seek is everlasting life, which must
be cultivated. Just as, therefore, a king guards his
material earth against enemy invasion, so should
he guard the earth of his own body, lest the Devil
snatch away the goods of the earth, that is, the

endowments of the body and the soul.

Just as in the world there are many kinds of inhabitants, among whom some are rulers, as princes; some enforces, as soldiers; others, subjects, ordinary men, so in the world of his body, the king should order the different tasks of the three activities: the activities of the reason, which rule; the activities of the senses, which enforce [that rule]; the activities of the flesh, which are subject to that rule.* And just as it befits a prince to work for the peace of this material earth, that is, to preserve the tranquillity of peace, so it is said to the princes of this world: 'Be instructed'—that is, be instructed in the lowly nature of your flesh—'you who judge the earth'— that is, you who in your own bodies condemn what is earthy.

Cf. Misc. 8.

What will your spirit say to you then, O prince of the earth, when it, a pauper, will judge you on the Day of Judgement, if you have ruled your sphere ill, and unjustly judged the poor?

[189]

O king, reckon not the honor of your princedom but rather bear in mind that earthly honor is not natural, but a matter of fortune, for their slippery mischance proves it true that such are not honors; their mutability shows their vanity. Many kings are borne to their graves with funeral honors and their bodies are borne with a certain superficial jubilation to the sepulchre, but their wretched souls are tormented miserably in hell, surrounded by a horrible rabble of demons. Where is then your secular honor, where the breath of popular favor, the throng of your household, the worldly riches, the nobility of birth, the offspring of your posterity, the beauty of your wife? Those things are of no profit to wretched souls after death—indeed, they only increase their grief.

CHAPTER XLIII: TO CLOISTERED RELIGIOUS[1]

Scripture, speaking to cloistered religious, says: 'See how good and how sweet it is for brothers to dwell together in unity!'* And elsewhere the Psalmist in the person of the monk says: 'I have asked one thing of the Lord, and this I desire, that I may dwell in the house of the Lord'.* For in moral philosophy unity is glossed with oft-repeated praises. In theology, it is not valued less than the least of the sacraments. Without spiritual unity, grace is not to be had in the present, nor glory to be conferred in the future. Without unity, all religion is but a breath, heavenly love grows cold, faith itself perishes and obedience fails.

Unity produces harmony in the divine, in angels concord, and in the churches obedience. For there is a unity above the heavens, a heavenly unity, and a unity beneath the heavens. The unity above the heavens lies in the concord of the Trinity, where there is a unifying and a united unity. The unifying and united unity is the Holy Spirit, who unites the Father with the Son, whence he is called: One with the Father and the Son,* and elsewhere he is said to be the kiss and love of the Father and the Son.** And he is unity united, for he is united to Father and Son in having the divine nature. Unity unifying, not united, is the divine nature itself, which unites the three Persons to each other, but is not itself united to them, for it is not itself a Person. Unity united but not unifying is the Father, for he is united with the Son and the Holy Spirit, but neither of them is united in him, but

Ps 133:1

Ps 27:4

*From Nunc sancte nobis spiritus, the hymn at Terce.
**Cf. William of St Thierry, Cant 95 (CF 6:78).*

1.   For lack of an English equivalent, *claustralis* 'cloister–dweller' has been translated generally as 'monk'.

through him. Of the unity unifying and united, it is also said: 'Now unto us, O Holy Spirit, who is one with the Father and the Son.'* Of unity not united is also said: 'Unity in majesty'. Of unity united, not unifying, Hilary says: 'In the Father is unity', and so forth.*

Terce hymn.

*Perhaps De Trinitate Bk 8, or De synodis 34.

But heavenly unity, that is, harmony among angels, is also a threefold unity: unity of nature, unity of grace, unity of glory. Unity of nature, for all are ministering spirits; unity of grace, for all are strengthened by grace; unity of glory, for all are glorified in eternal blessedness. In this threefold unity is diversity among these ministers in merit and in their knowledge of the hidden mysteries. For there is there a harmony of disharmonies, concordant discord, diverse unity, united diversity, consenting dissent, diversity unifying.

[190]

Unity beneath heaven should lie in the Church, and this, too, is threefold: unity of faith, unity of charity, unity of obedience; so the lesser should obey the greater, and the greater should behave with moderation towards the lesser. To signify the merit of this unity, one going down into the pool was healed.* One who was the son of a widow was revived.* The Ark was topped by one cubit.* One was sent to announce the victory to David.* One told Job of the death of his sons, in which one alone escaped danger.* Unity embraces all things which belong to the condition of the Church, and singularity underlies all: for there is one Lord, one faith, one baptism,* one law, one King, one Church, one grace, one glory.

Jn 5:8
1 K 17:22
Gn 6:16
2 S 18:24
Jb 1:19

Eph 4:5

And thus likewise among religious there should be a threefold unity: unity of religion; unity of possession; unity of charity. Unity of religion, that they be uniform in habit, in provisions, in vigils, in fasting. But some irregulars except themselves from the rule

of this unity, desiring to lie on softer beds, to be
present at fewer vigils, to eat more delicate meals,
to practise silence little or not at all. Certain monks,
indeed, stand out in some way by their cheap habit,
or by dusting themselves with dirt, or by a certain
elegance in the disposition of their limbs, for either
they put their feet into narrow shoes, or they tie up
their sleeves, or they turn back their hoods behind
their ears. Also they yearn for more delicate food as
far as they can, and if they cannot change its ingre-
dients, at least they change its appearance as far
as they can. If someone wishes to prepare beans, or
any other plain food one way, another wants it
another way. Some break the silence—if not in words,
then by signs—so that they light little torches of con-
versation with their many signs. Some either miss
vigils, or skip them altogether.

There should, too, be unity in possession, that all
things may be held in common, for the monk should
have nothing for his own, either in possessing things
or in exercising his own will. Let them understand
by the example of Ananias, who died at the feet of
Peter for holding back something as his own,* that
they should hold nothing for their own, for he held
back something for himself. For the instruction of
cloistered monks, the Lord says: 'Unless a man renounce all he possesses, he cannot be my disciple'.*
Nor does it suffice to renounce possessions in fact,
unless they are renounced in the will, whence Peter
says of this renunciation of the will: 'Behold, we have
given up all and followed you'.* Therefore the monk
who desires to have possessions looks back with Lot's
wife,* takes his hand from the plough** and, with
Dinah, Jacob's daughter, covets the stranger's adorn-
ments.* He, then, who steals from the common property anything for himself, takes the place of the thief

Ac 5:5

Lk 14:33

Mt 19:27

*Gn 19:26
**Cf. Lk 9:62

Cf. Gn 34:3

and traitor Judas.

O monk, you who renounced many things in the world, do not return to the world by desiring one miserable farthing. Let not the yen for one farthing ensnare you, whom a treasure-house of wealth did not deceive! Fear lest the devil's snare catch you by little things, when it did not deceive you by great.

[191]

A monk should also cast away his own will, so that, just as there is a community in religion, so there may be one in will, that not only may all things be held in common in the archives, but also by agreement. Thus everyone may agree in a single will, everyone agree in a single charity, and it may be truly said of them: 'They had one heart and one soul'.*

Ac 4:32

The cloistered are bound too, to have unity in charity, that they may find their own advancement in the advancement of their neighbors, and may grieve at another's loss as at their own. Let the wiser instruct the less experienced, the healthy sympathize with the sick, and he who is uninjured rejoice with him who is well. Thus the cloistered life may be the image of the heavenly life, so that just as in eternal life there will be equal joy amid unequal brightness' so in the cloistered, let there be a single bond of love amid unequal charity.* Because of this threefold unity, the cloister-dweller is called a 'monk',[2] as one who is the guardian of unity. Now if he does not preserve the first unity, he becomes an anomaly; if he does not preserve the second, an apostate; if he does not preserve the third, a schismatic.

Cf. 1 Co 15:41

claritas—charitas.

Let there be in the convent a unifying and united unity, that is a superior, uniting his subordinates by authority, and united to them by charity. Let there be unity united, not unifying, that is, let the subordinate who, even if he does not unite others, nevertheless join himself to others in charity. Let there be

---

2.   *Monachus* derives etymologically from the Greek *monas*, one.

there a unity unifying but not united, that is the charity which, even though it unites monks, yet does not attach itself firmly to any one in particular in this life. Let there be among them the unity of nature, that they may love unity for its own sake; let there be the unity of grace, that they may lend one another the grace which has been given them; let there be the unity of glory, that with one hope they may tend towards the glory of eternal life. Let there be unity of faith, lest they be heretics; unity of charity, lest they be schismatics. Let there be unity of hope, lest they be stubborn, that it may be said of them in particular: 'Lo, how good (in the opinion of men) and how joyous (in devotion of mind) it is for brothers to live together in unity* (of religion, in singleness of possessions, in singleness of love), so that they may come to that unity of which the prophet speaks: 'One thing have I asked of the Lord'.*

Ps 133:1

CHAPTER XLIV: TO PRIESTS

To priests the Lord says: 'You are the salt of the earth. If the salt loses it savor, how shall it be seasoned?'* Salt has four properties: it makes the ground infertile; it flavors food; it protects meat from decay, and it keeps worms out of meat. These four come together in the spiritual salt, that is, in the priest, who should plough the earth of his people—that is, plough up their earthly thoughts with the ploughshare of his preaching—lest they sprout the thorns and thistles of the vices, and thus he should make the land infertile for evil works. His own land, that is, his own flesh, he is bound to make infertile to the vices and he must preserve his flesh from decay,

Mt 5:13

that is, keep it free of dissipation and gluttony. Dissipation is appropriately compared with decay, for just as decay corrupts flesh and makes it stink, so dissipation makes a man stink by notoriety, his flesh stink by its uncleanness, and the man himself stink by his bad conscience. Drunkenness, too, may be compared with decay, for through drunkenness a man is corrupted in body, is destroyed by decay, and swiftly tends to become nothing.

[192]

He should guard his flesh against worms, lest the flesh beget evil thoughts or stray into inordinate desires. He must, too, salt the food of Holy Scripture with diligent study, for Holy Scripture seems tasteless in certain parts unless it is read with diligent study. He should salt the food of the Eucharist with good works, for unless he is worthy to taste the food which is sweet in itself it tastes bitter, and what is medicine to the righteous is wormwood to the unrighteous. He must salt the food of his teaching with the example of a good life, lest he be despised for the quality of his life, and his preaching be deservedly spurned.

But if that salt becomes tasteless, how is it to be seasoned? The salt of priesthood becomes tasteless in three ways: through ignorance, through negligence, through greed, for the priests of our day are old men

*Seneca Ep 36.4
cf. Ch. 38 above.
†Cf. Peter of Blois,
Ep 6; PL 217:18
*Jr 2:8

who are school-children,* boys a hundred years old,† of whom the Lord says through the prophet: 'Those who administered the law did not know Me'.* How can such men salt others? For they know how to instruct neither themselves nor others. It often happens, when priests, through their own fault, do not have the light of knowledge, that through their ignorance they put a stumbling-block before their followers. Therefore the Lord says: 'If a blind man leads another

Lk 6:39

blind man, both will fall into a ditch'.* If the [priests] are tasteless, in the error of ignorance, who will season them with the salt of wisdom, when they should teach rather than be taught, instruct, and not be instructed? When the leaders have no-one above themselves to correct them, and those who are more prudent have no-one to instruct them, they are made tasteless through neglectfulness, for negligence produces indifference in all their works, and destroys the fruit of their works. There is no devotion in their psalms, no thoughtfulness in their reading, in their exhortations to penitence no diligence, no care in celebrating Mass; in their direction of their flocks no discretion; in their good works no effort.

But if they are tasteless, how shall they be seasoned? Who can save them from the precipice of such negligence? Who can season them with the flavor of diligence? They are tasteless through greed, for they sell Christ himself for money and thus take the place of Judas the traitor. They offer baptisms for a price, and put up funerals for sale. They caress the vices of their subordinates in order to earn money; they fawn upon the vices, to fill their purses. Such salt is not offered to God in sacrifice, but thrown away; it is trodden underfoot and cast on the dungheap. For such priests are not worthy to offer themselves to God in sacrifice, nor do they season their sacrifices with the salt of wisdom, but they perform the sacraments unworthily, they consecrate unworthily, and so the salt is taken from the sacrifice, since God forbids a sacrifice to be offered without salt; so the salt is thrown away.

Such priests, even if they are numbered among the Church by name, are not members by God's pleasure[1] or their merit, but they deserve to be trodden underfoot. The feet are their subordinates for whom the

---

1.   A play on words: *nomen; numerus; numen.*

[193]

priests of the Church are bound to provide, lest they set before them a stumbling-block of guilt on the road of this life. By these feet are wicked priests trodden underfoot, for when their subordinates see that they are clouded with ignorance and feeble from idleness, that those whom they should hold up as a model of the good, they have as an example of evil, and that those who should be the model for their flocks are a joke to their people—then the salt is thrown on the dung-heap. For such priests stink with the stench of infamy; they decay in the corruption of sin, and rot in the dung of habitual evil-doing. Let there be salt then in priests, and let them be at peace among themselves.

CHAPTER XLV: TO THOSE WHO ARE MARRIED

The Apostle Paul says: 'Let each man have his own wife, to prevent fornication',* and, again: 'It is better to marry than to burn'.* Instituting marriage in paradise, the Lord said: 'Increase and multiply'.* In the Gospel, too, Christ says: 'What God has joined together, let man not separate'.*

1 Co 7:2
1 Co 7:9
Gen 1:28

Mt 19:6,
Mk 10:9

How great is the dignity of marriage, which had its beginning in paradise, which takes away the sinfulness from incontinence, which embraces within itself a heavenly sacrament which keeps men faithful to the marriage-bed; which provides between spouses a companionship for life; which redeems the children from the reproach [of illegitimacy]; which exculpates carnal intercourse. In this state were the Patriarchs saved, and in this condition were certain of the Apostles chosen.

How great is the virtue of this sacrament! If anyone were in danger of sliding over the precipice into
dissipation or incontinence, he is held secure in honorable marriage. O how does he who violates the fidelity
of the marriage-bed sweep aside that honor! When he
leaves the marriage-bed and commits adultery in another bed, he defiles the sacrament—insofar as he can.
He pollutes his own body, sins against his own soul,
sunders the unity of matrimony, breaks the vows of
wedlock.

O how great is the danger of adultery! A man sins
against God and gives offence to his neighbor; often
murder is committed, the legitimate son is often
disinherited, daughter frequently weds father and the
sister her brother. Adultery is usually the cause of
manifold disgrace; because of adultery, David sank to
murder and Reuben fell under his father's curse.†

*2 S 11
†Gn 35:22 & 49:3-4

In commendation of marriage: Christ was born of
a betrothed woman, and his gifts were bestowed at
the wedding at Cana in Galilee.* But although it per-
mits carnal intercourse without sin, yet this is to be
practised for the begetting of children, not for the
pleasure of the flesh. Therefore let fleshly union be
controlled by the reason of a proper time and a proper
place, and by religious duty.

Jn 2

Let a man observe a spiritual marriage between
the body and the soul, that the flesh, like a woman,
may obey the spirit, and the spirit, like a man, may
rule his flesh as if it were a woman. Let there be in it
fidelity to the marriage-bed; lest the flesh, refusing
to be ruled by the spirit, commit adultery with the
world, or the reason, itself tempted by the allurements of the flesh, commit fornication with them: for
it is said that he who loves his wife too passionately
is an adulterer.

Let there be in it the hope of begetting children,

[194]

that is, the intention of performing a good work. Let
there be in it the sacrament of spiritual conjoining,
and let good works be begotten as if they were
children. Let there be both an intercourse and a
copulation of the flesh and of the rational spirit.

CHAPTER XLVI: OF WIDOWS

Concerning widows, the Apostle says: 'To those
who are unmarried and widows: it is good for them if
they remain as I am myself',* that is, chaste. And elsewhere: 'But I wish all men were as I am myself',* that
is, that they were continent. Although the married
state is good, the widowed state carries fewer encumbrances.

For in marriage, there is the difficulty of remaining
faithful to the marriage-bed, and the problem of honor-
ing its vows and moderating carnal intercourse. [In mar-
riage] there is the effort of concern over family
matters, the burden of bringing up children, the pain
of the wife in giving birth, and her discomfort while
she carries her child in her womb. There, the wife is
subject to the power of her husband, even if he is
violent. There the husband must worry about his
wife committing adultery. The power for the married
man is not absolute: there are ungoverned impulses,
even if venial ones. Therefore a widow should not go
a second time into marriage, for second marriages raise
the suspicion of dissipation and furnish evidence of
incontinence.

Widowed by an earthly husband, let a woman take
a heavenly Bridegroom; where there is child-bearing
without labor, birth without pain, where strict righteousness is protected. Here, God is life eternal,

1 Co 7:8
1 Co 7:7

conceiving is ordered by the will, the giving of birth is
good works, desire is charity, faithfulness to the
marriage-bed is long-suffering, the sacrament is
the issue of the sacrament, the bed is chastity, seeing
is contemplation, speaking is prayer, touch is eternal
love, a kiss is peace of mind and there carnal intercourse is eternal joy.

O widow, if you seek an example for the state of
widowhood, you will find the model of widowhood
in Anna the Prophetess.* She, by the merit of her
continence, earned the gift of prophecy, and because
of her chastity, she deserved to see the Messiah.
Widowhood, then, invites you to be chaste, like the
faithful turtle-dove, which, when it has lost its mate,
seeks neither to love nor to be loved. If she loses her
mate, she sits neither on the green bough nor on the
growing plant. [This bird] advises you at the moment
of your widowhood, O widow, to despise the flower
of this ageing world, to set at nought the burgeoning
of worldly delight. O widow, if you involve yourself
with an earthly husband, you serve your heavenly
spouse less freely. For 'No-one can serve two masters'* and while you incline towards the flesh, you
incline less towards the spirit.

Lk 2:36

Mt 6:24

CHAPTER XLVII: TO VIRGINS

To virgins it is said: 'I espoused you to a single
husband, so that I might present you as a pure virgin
to Christ'.* And the prophet says: 'Hear, daughter
and behold' and so on.* O maiden, you who are set
apart by the seal of virginity, by your title of modesty,
do not betray that which nature has especially en-
trusted to you and by which she freely sets you apart.
Do not lose for a moment's pleasure that which can

2 Co 11:2

Ps 45:11

in no way be restored. This is the treasure-house of
nature, and [the treasure], once lost, cannot be
recovered. This is the flower which burst
into bloom once, never to bloom again.
This is the star which, when it sets, does not rise
again. This is the gift for whose loss there is no
recompense. Because this alone you cannot regain,
you should preserve it the more carefully. In this
respect only, man is like the angels while he lives in
the flesh; in this respect alone, man conquers himself.
This gift preserves the integrity of reputation, and
guards the flesh from defilement.

Ps 45:11 'Hear, therefore, daughter',* not only with the ear
of the body, but also with the ear of your mind, and
see with the eye of the heart, that you may understand; 'incline your ear'—your bodily ear—that you
Ibid. may obey, and so 'forget your own people'.* The
people is the concourse of carnal thoughts which
suggests to the virgin that she should experience
marriage, be happy in the embraces of a husband,
bear children and enjoy the delights of the flesh.

But forget such a people, for it is the people of
Babylon, the race of confusion which tries to take
captive the daughter of Sion. 'Forget, too, your
Ibid. father's house.'* Your father is the spark of sin
which begot you, which brought you forth from
your mother, whose house and habitation is lust,
in which that 'spark' rules, commands, controls,
and gives orders.

Ibid. 'And so the King shall desire your beauty'*—that
King, indeed, who is King of Kings and Lord of
Lords, of whom it is said: 'In the north is the City of
Ps 48:2 the Great King',* and elsewhere: 'The earth is the
Ps 24:1 Lord's and the fulness thereof'.* O virgin, if you
wish to marry an earthly husband because he is in the
flower of youth, consider how death will pluck away

[195]

Reading deflorescit that flower, or else it will wither* in any case in the
for efflorescit.   winter of old age.

Marry, then, that Husband who alone has immortality, 'in whom is no change, nor the shadow of any
Jm 1:17   alteration'.* If you wish to marry an earthly husband
because of his wealth, consider how deceptive and
transitory they are, for either they pass away in this
life, or they disappear in any case in death. Marry then
him in whom are incomparable treasures and change-
less riches, 'which no thief may steal, nor rust may
Mt 6:20   corrupt'.* If, however, you wish to marry an earthly
husband because he is outstanding in handsomeness,
consider that either sickness may waste or old age
wipe out that handsomeness, or that the finger of
death will in any case blot it out. Marry then him at
Cf. Jdt 10:7,14   whose beauty the sun and moon marvel.* If you wish
to marry an earthly husband because of his noble
ancestry, marry him of whom it is said: 'Who shall
Is 53:8   tell his ancestry?'* If you wish to marry an earthly
husband for worldly honor or earthly position, consi-
der how even the loftiest have been denied standing
for long and those burdened under too heavy a
weight have fallen. Therefore marry him of whom it
Jb 9:4   is said: 'Who resists his power?'* and elsewhere: 'Of
Lk 1:33   his kingdom there shall be no end'.*

The chapter which follows in Migne, XLVIII Ad somno-
lentes, *is, in fact, the first of the sermons in Alan's* Liber
Sermonum. *It is a sermon for the first Sunday of Advent
and does not belong to the* Art of Preaching. *See J. B.
Schneyer,* Repertorium der lateinischen Sermones des
Mittelalters A–D *(Munster/W., 1969) p. 70, no. 13, and
my note ot the sermon in the forthcoming translation of
Alan's sermons.*

ABBREVIATIONS

Ad Fratres   Pseudo-Augustine *Sermons*, PL 40.1231–58. On
in Eremo   these see J. P. Bonnes 'Un de plus grands prédicateurs
                du xiie siècle, Geoffroy de Louroux dit Geoffroy
                Babion' R Bén 56 (1945–6) 174–215.

AP   The *Art of Preaching*

Asspt   Bernard of Clairvaux, Sermon on the Assumption

BS   The *Books of Sermons*

Csi   Bernard of Clairvaux, Five Books on Consideration

DDC   Augustine, *De doctrine christiana*

Enchr.   *Enchiridion Sexti; The Sentences of Sextus*, ed. H. Chad-
                wick (Cambridge, 1959).

Miller   J. M. Miller, *Readings in Mediaeval Rhetoric* (Indiana,
                1973)

Misc.   *Miscellaneous Sermons*

PL   J.P. Migne, *Patrologia Latina*

Texts   M. T. d'Alverny, *Alain de Lille, Textes inédits* (Paris,
                1965).

CISTERCIAN PUBLICATIONS INC.

Titles Listing

THE CISTERCIAN FATHERS SERIES

THE WORKS OF BERNARD OF CLAIRVAUX

THE WORKS OF WILLIAM OF SAINT THIERRY

THE WORKS OF AELRED OF RIEVAULX

THE WORKS OF GILBERT OF HOYLAND

OTHER EARLY CISTERCIAN WRITERS

THE CISTERCIAN STUDIES SERIES

*   out of print